Solving Enterprise Applications Performance Puzzles

Solving Enterprise Applications Performance Puzzles

Queuing Models to the Rescue

Leonid Grinshpan

IEEE PRESS

A John Wiley & Sons, Inc., Publication

For general information on our other products and services or for technical support, please
contact our Customer Care Department within the United States at (800) 762-2974, outside the
United States at (317) 572-3993 or fax (317) 572-4002.

Wiley also publishes its books in a variety of electronic formats. Some content that appears in
print may not be available in electronic formats. For more information about Wiley products,
visit our website at www.wiley.com.

Library of Congress Cataloging-in-Publication Data:

Grinshpan, L. A. (Leonid Abramovich)
    Solving enterprise applications performance puzzles : queuing models to the rescue /
Leonid Grinshpan. – 1st ed.
        p. cm.
    ISBN 978-1-118-06157-2 (pbk.)
1. Queuing theory.   I. Title.
    T57.9.G75 2011
    658.4'034–dc23

                                    2011020123

10 9 8 7 6 5 4 3 2 1

Contents

Acknowledgments

My career as a computer professional started in the USSR in the 1960s when I was admitted to engineering college and decided to major in an obscure area officially called "Mathematical and Computational Tools and Devices." Time proved that I made the right bet—computers became the major driver of civilization's progress, and (for better or for worse) they have developed into a vital component of our social lives. As I witnessed permanent innovations in my beloved occupation, I was always intrigued by the question: What does it take for such a colossal complex combination of hardware and software to provide acceptable services to its users (which is the ultimate goal of any application, no matter what task it carries out), what is its architecture, software technology, user base, etc.? My research lead me to queuing theory; in a few years I completed a dissertation on queuing models of computer systems and received a Ph.D. from the Academy of Science of the USSR.

Navigating the charted and uncharted waters of science and engineering, I wrote many articles on computer system modeling that were published in leading Soviet scientific journals and reprinted in the United States, as well as a book titled *Mathematical Methods for Queuing Network Models of Computer Systems*. I contributed to the scientific community by volunteering for many years as a reviewer for the computer science section of *Mathematical Reviews*, published by American Mathematical Society.

My professional life took me through the major generations of architectures and technologies, and I was fortunate to have multiple incarnations along the way: hardware engineer, software developer, microprocessor system programmer, system architect, performance analyst, project manager, scientist, etc. Each "embodiment" contributed to my vision of a computer system as an amazingly complex universe living by its own laws that have to be discovered in order to ensure that the system delivers on expectations.

When perestroika transformed the Soviet Union to Soviet Disunion, I came to work in the United States. For the past 15 years as an Oracle consultant, I was hands-on engaged in performance tuning and sizing of enterprise applications for Oracle's customers and prospects.

I executed hundreds of projects for corporations such as Dell, Citibank, Verizon, Clorox, Bank of America, AT&T, Best Buy, Aetna, Halliburton, etc. Many times I was requested to save failing performance projects in the shortest time possible, and every time the reason for the failure was a lack of understanding of the fundamental relationships among enterprise application architecture, workload generated by users, and software design by engineers who executed system sizing and tuning. I began collecting enterprise application performance problems, and over time I found that I had a sufficient assortment to write a book that could assist my colleagues with problem troubleshooting.

I want to express my gratitude to people as well as acknowledge the facts and the entities that directly or indirectly contributed to this book. My appreciation goes to:

- Knowledgeable and honest Soviet engineers and scientists I was very fortunate to work with; they always remained *Homo sapiens* despite tremendous pressure from the system to make them *Homo sovieticus*.
- The Soviet educational system with its emphasis on mathematics and physics.
- The overwhelming scarcity of everything except communist demagogy in the Soviet Union; as the latter was of no use, the former was a great enabler of innovative approaches to problem solving (for example, if the computer is slow and has limited memory, the only way to meet requirements is to devise a very efficient algorithm).
- U.S. employers who opened for me the world of enterprise applications filled with performance puzzles.
- Performance engineers who drove tuning and sizing projects to failures—I learned how they did it, and I did what was necessary to prevent it; along the way I collected real-life cases.
- Reviewers who reconsidered their own priorities and accepted publishers' proposals to examine raw manuscripts; the recipes they recommended made it edible.
- My family for the obvious and the most important reason—because of their presence, I have those to love and those to take care of.

L.G.

Preface

In this chapter: why the book was written; what it is about; its targeted audience; and the book's organization.

WHY I WROTE THIS BOOK

Poorly performing enterprise applications are the weakest links in a corporation's management chains, causing delays and disruptions of critical business functions. In trying to strengthen the links, companies spend dearly on applications tuning and sizing; unfortunately, the only deliverables of many of such ventures are lost investment as well as the ruined credibility of computer professionals who carry out failed projects.

In my opinion, the root of the problem is twofold. Firstly, the performance engineering discipline does not treat enterprise applications as a unified compound object that has to be tuned in its entirety; instead it targets separate components of enterprise applications (databases, software, networks, Web servers, application servers, hardware appliances, Java Virtual Machine, etc.).

Secondly, the body of knowledge for performance engineering consists of disparate and isolated tips and recipes on bottleneck troubleshooting and system sizing and is guided by intuitional and "trial and error" approaches. Not surprisingly, the professional community has categorized it as an art form—you can find a number of books that prominently place application performance trade in the category of "art form," based on their titles.

What greatly contributes to the problem are corporations' misguided efforts that are directed predominantly toward information technology (IT) department business optimization while typically ignoring application performance management (APM). Because performance indicators of IT departments and enterprise applications differ—hardware utilization on one side and transaction time on another—the perfect readings of the former do not equate to business user satisfaction with the latter. Moreover, IT departments do not monitor software bottlenecks that degrade transaction time; ironically, being undetected, they make IT feel better because software bottlenecks bring down hardware utilization.

A few years ago I decided to write a book that put a scientific foundation under the performance engineering of enterprise applications based on their queuing models. I have successfully used the modeling approach to identify and solve performance issues; I hope a book on modeling methodology can be as helpful to the performance engineering community as it was of great assistance to me for many years.

SUBJECT

Enterprise applications are the information backbones of today's corporations and support vital business functions such as operational management, supply chain maintenance, customer relationship administration, business intelligence, accounting, procurement logistics, etc. Acceptable performance of enterprise applications is critical for a company's day-to-day operations as well as for its profitability. The high complexity of enterprise applications makes achieving satisfactory performance a nontrivial task. Systematic implementation of performance tuning and capacity planning processes is the only way to ensure high quality of the services delivered by applications to their business users.

Application tuning is a course of action that aims at identifying and fixing bottlenecks in production systems. Capacity planning (also known as application sizing) takes place on the application predeployment stage as well as when existing production systems have to be scaled to accommodate growth in the number of users and volume of data. Sizing delivers the estimates of hardware architecture that will be capable of providing the requested service quality for the anticipated workload. Tuning and sizing require understanding of a business process supported by the application, as well as application, hardware, and operating systems functionality. Both tasks are challenging, effort-intense, and their execution is time constrained as they are tightly woven into all phases of an application's life in the corporate environment:

Phase of Enterprise Application Life in the Corporate Environment	Role of Tuning and Sizing
(1) Sales	Capacity planning to determine hardware architecture to host an application
(2) Application deployment	Setting up hardware infrastructure according to capacity planning recommendations, application customization, and population with business data
(3) Performance testing	Performance tuning based on application performance under an emulated workload
(4) Application live in production mode	Monitoring application performance, tuning application to avoid bottlenecks due to real workload fluctuations
(5) Scaling production application	Capacity planning to accommodate an increase in the number of users and data volume

Enterprise applications permanently evolve as they have to stay in sync with the ever-changing businesses they support. That creates a constant need for application tuning and sizing due to the changes in the number of users, volume of data, and complexity of business transactions.

Enterprise applications are very intricate objects. Usually they are hosted on server farms and provide services to a large number of business users connected to the system from geographically distributed offices over corporate and virtual private networks. Unlike other technical and nontechnical systems, there is no way for human beings to watch, listen, touch, taste, or smell enterprise applications that run data crunching processes. What can remediate the situation is application instrumentation—a technology that enables the collection of application performance metrics. To great regret, the state of the matter is that instrumented enterprise applications are mostly dreams that did not come true. Life's bare realities are significantly trickier, and performance engineering teams more often than not feel like they are dealing with evasive objects astronomers call "black holes," those regions of space where gravity is so powerful that nothing, not even light, can escape its pull. This makes black holes unavailable to our senses; however, astronomers managed to develop models explaining the processes and events inside black holes; the models are even capable of forecasting black holes' evolution. Models are ubiquitous in physics, chemistry, mathematics, and many other areas of knowledge where human imagination has to be unleashed in order to explain and predict activities and events that escape our senses.

In this book we build and analyze enterprise application queuing models that help interpret in human understandable ways happenings in systems that serve multiple requests from concurrent users traveling across a "tangle wood" of servers, networks, and numerous appliances. Models are powerful methodological instruments that greatly facilitate the solving of performance puzzles. A lack of adequate representation of internal processes in enterprise applications can be blamed for the failure of many performance tuning and sizing projects.

This book establishes a model-based methodological foundation for the tuning and sizing of enterprise applications in all stages of their life cycle within a corporation. Introduced modeling concepts and methodology "visualize" and explain processes inside an application, as well as the provenance of system bottlenecks. Models help to frame the quest for performance puzzle solutions as scientific projects that eliminate guesswork and guesstimates. The book contains models of different enterprise applications architectures and phenomena; analyses of the models that uncover connections, and correlations that are not obvious among workload, hardware architecture, and software parameters.

In the course of this work we consider enterprise applications as entities that consist of three components: business-oriented software, hosting hardware infrastructure, and operating systems.

The book's modeling concepts are based on representation of the complex computer systems as queuing networks. The abstract nature of a queuing network helps us get through the system complexity that obstructs clear thinking; it facilitates the identification of events and objects, and the connections among them that cause performance deficiencies. The described methodology is applicable to the tuning and sizing of enterprise applications that serve different industries.

AUDIENCE

The book targets multifaceted teams of specialists working in concert on sizing, deployment, tuning, and maintaining enterprise applications. Computer system performance analysts, system architects, as well as developers who adapt applications at their deployment stage to a corporation's business logistics can benefit by making the book's methodology part of their toolbox.

Two additional categories of team members will find valuable information here: business users and product managers. A chapter on workload assists business users to define application workload by describing how they carry out their business tasks. System sizing methodology is of interest to product managers—they can use it to include in product documentation application sizing guides with estimates of the hardware needed to deploy applications. Such guides also are greatly sought by sales professionals who work with prospects and customers.

Students majoring in computer science will find numerous examples of queuing models of enterprise applications as well as an introduction into model solving. That paves the way into the limitless world of computer system modeling; curious minds immersed in that world will find plenty of opportunities to expand and enrich the foundations of performance engineering.

In order to enhance communication between team members, this book introduces a number of analogies that visualize objects or processes (for example, representation of a business transaction as a car or a queuing network as a highway network). As the author's experience has indicated, the analogies often serve as "eye openers" for decision-making executives and an application's business users; they help performance engineers to communicate with nontechnical but influential project stakeholders. The analogies are efficient vehicles delivering the right message and facilitating an understanding by all project participants of the technicalities.

Here is what a reader will take away from the book:

- An understanding of the root causes of poor performance of enterprise applications based on their queuing network models
- Learning that enterprise application performance troubleshooting encompasses three components that have to be addressed as a whole: hardware, software, and workload
- A clear understanding of an application's workload characterization and that doing it wrong ruins entire performance tuning and sizing projects
- Quick identification of hardware bottlenecks

- Quick identification of software bottlenecks
- Quick identification of memory bottlenecks
- Scientific methodology of application sizing
- Methodology of realistic estimates of virtual platforms capacity
- Understanding the impacts on performance by various technological solutions (for example, deployment architectures, geographical distribution of users, networks connection latencies, remote terminal services, loads balancing, server farms, transaction parallelization, etc)

Some degree of imagination is needed to embrace modeling concepts and thinking promoted by this book as ammunition for solving performance puzzles. In addition to imagination, it is supposed that a standard performance practitioner's body of knowledge is possessed by the reader. A note to the readers who are not friendly with mathematics: this book includes a limited number of basic and simple formulas sufficient to understand modeling principles and modeling results. It does not impose on the reader mathematical intricacies of model solving; the book is entirely dedicated to performance-related issues and challenges that are discovered and explained using modeling concepts and methodology. The book is not by any means a call to arm every performance professional with ultimate knowledge of model building and solving techniques; while such knowledge is highly desirable, our goal is to promote usage of modeling concepts while solving essential performance analyst tasks.

ORGANIZATION

We use modeling concepts to visualize, demystify, explain, and help to solve essential performance analyst tasks. This is what you will find in each chapter:

Chapter 1 outlines specifics of enterprise applications and introduces queuing networks as their models. It defines transactions and clarifies how they travel across computer systems and what contributes to their processing time. Transaction time and transaction profile are explained in detail.

Chapter 2 contains an overview of the procedures of building and solving enterprise application models. It highlights basic concepts of queuing theory and describes how to define a model's components, topology, input data, as well as how to calibrate the model and interpret modeling results. The chapter reviews commercial and open source software that helps to analyze queuing models.

Chapter 3 is dedicated to workload characterization and demonstrates its fundamental importance for application tuning and sizing. It explores transaction rate and user think time, and workload deviations and their impact on application performance as well as user concurrency. The chapter discusses an approach to business process analysis that delivers workload metrics.

Chapter 4 is focused on identification and fixing hardware bottlenecks caused by insufficient capacity of servers, CPUs, I/O systems, and network components. Hardware scaling techniques are modeled and examined.

Chapter 5 analyzes the impact of operating system overhead on transaction time and hardware utilization.

Chapter 6 highlights identification and remediation of software bottlenecks rooted in limited numbers of threads, database connections, user sessions, as well as in a lack of memory and application design flows.

Chapter 7 evaluates factors defining performance and capacity of virtual environments and explains how to implement capacity planning of virtual environments.

Chapter 8 describes the model-based methodology of application sizing that provides better prediction of hardware capacity than empirical estimates.

Chapter 9 demonstrates how to model and evaluate performance implications of different application deployment patterns (remote users, remote sessions, various operating systems, thick clients, load balancing, and server farms) as well as multithreading software architecture.

A few final notes before we start. In this book we consider enterprise application from the business user's point of view: in corporate lingo, the enterprise application is an object that supports implementation of critical corporate functions and includes three components: business-oriented software, the hardware infrastructure that hosts it, as well as operating systems.

When referring to performance counters we are mostly using their names according to Windows Performance Monitor terminology. Similar counters exist in all UNIX operating systems, but their names might differ, and a reader should consult documentation to find the matching equivalent.

LEONID GRINSHPAN

## CHAPTER 1

Queuing Networks as Applications Models

In this chapter: characteristics of enterprise applications and their key performance indicators; what is application sizing and tuning; why queuing models are representative abstractions of enterprise applications; what is transaction response time and transaction profile.

1.1. ENTERPRISE APPLICATIONS—WHAT DO THEY HAVE IN COMMON?

Enterprise applications have a number of characteristics essential from a performance engineering perspective.

1. Enterprise applications support vital corporate business functions, and their performance is critical for successful execution of business tasks. Consider as an example the failure of a company to deliver a timely quarterly earnings report to its shareholders and Wall Street due to a bottleneck in one of the system servers, which had crashed and brought the application down.

Solving Enterprise Applications Performance Puzzles: Queuing Models to the Rescue, First Edition. Leonid Grinshpan.
© 2012 Institute of Electrical and Electronics Engineers. Published 2012 by John Wiley & Sons, Inc.

2. Corporations inherently tend to grow by expanding their customer base, opening new divisions, releasing new products, as well as engaging in restructuring, mergers, and acquisitions. Business dynamics directly affects a number of application users, as well as the volume and structure of data loaded into databases. That means that tuning and sizing must be organic and indispensable components of the application life cycle, ensuring its adaptation to an ever-changing environment.

3. Each company is unique in terms of operational practice, customer base, product nomenclature, cost structure, and other aspects of business logistics; as such, enterprise applications cannot be deployed right after being purchased as they must undergo broad customization and be tested and tuned for performance before being released in production.

4. The typical enterprise application architecture represents server farms with users connected to the system from geographically distributed offices over corporate and virtual private networks.

5. Enterprise applications deal with much larger and complex data per a user's request as opposed to Internet applications because they sift through megabytes and even terabytes of business records and often implement massive online analytical processing (OLAP) in order to deliver business data rendered as reports, tables, sophisticated forms, and templates.

6. The number of enterprise application users is significantly lower than that of Internet application users since their user communities are limited to corporation business departments. That number can still be quite large, reaching thousands of users, but it never even comes close to millions as in the case of Internet applications.

7. End users work with enterprise applications not only through their browsers, as with Internet applications, but also through a variety of front-end programs (for example, Excel or Power-Point, as well as interface programs specifically designed for different business tasks). Often front-end programs do large processing of information that is delivered from servers before making it available to the users.

8. A significant factor influencing the workload of enterprise applications is the rate of the requests submitted by the users—a

number of requests per given time interval, usually per one work hour. Pacing defines an intensity of requests from the users and by the same token utilization of system resources.

Enterprise applications have a client-server architecture [1.1], where the user (client) works with a client program; through this program the user demands a service from a server program by sending a request over the corporate network (Fig. 1.1). The client program resides on the user's computer; the server program is hosted on a server.

Figure 1.1 represents a two-tier implementation of client-server architecture. Today's complex enterprise applications are hosted on multi-tier platforms; the most common is the three-tier platform (Fig. 1.2). The functional logic of the application is performed by software hosted on a middle tier; data are stored in the database tier.

Three-tier architecture has a fundamental performance advantage over the two-tier structure because it is *scalable*; that means it can support more users and a higher intensity of requests by increasing the number of servers and their capacity on a functional tier.

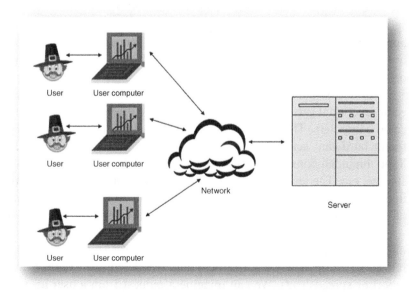

Figure 1.1. Client-server architecture.

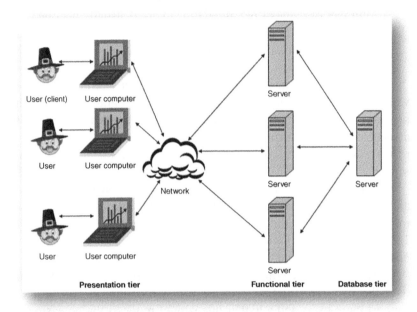

Figure 1.2. Three-tier architecture.

The next level of scalability can be achieved by separation of Web servers from the functional tier (Fig. 1.3). This is possible for enterprise applications where the presentation tier communicates to the system over the Internet. The Web server tier is scalable as well and can comprise multiple Web servers.

Ultimate scalability is delivered by network-like architecture where each functional service of the enterprise application is hosted on dedicated computers. This architecture is illustrated in Fig. 1.4, where different hardware servers host services like data integration, business logic, financial consolidation, report printing, data import/export, data storage, etc. The architecture in Fig. 1.4 can support practically unlimited growth in the number of business users and complexity or volume of data by deploying additional servers that host different services.

In a network of servers, a request from a user sequentially visits different servers and is processed on each one for some time until it returns to a user delivering business data (rendered, for example, as a report or spreadsheet). We can imagine a request from a user as a car traveling across network of highways with tollbooths. A tollboth is

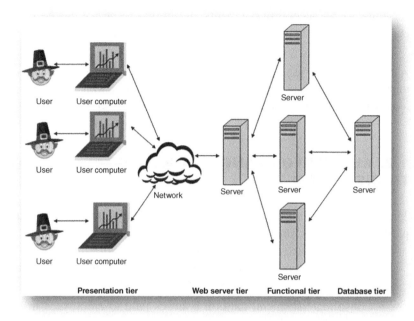

Figure 1.3. Four-tier architecture.

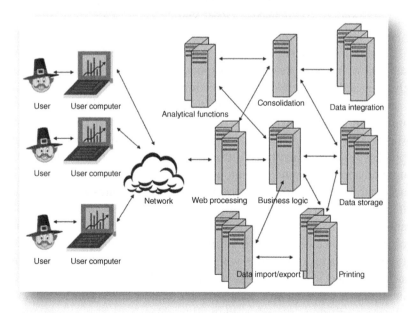

Figure 1.4. Network of servers.

serving cars by accepting payments and in that respect it can be compared to a hardware server working on users' requests.

A user's request to an application can be imagined as a car and a highway's tollbooth as a hardware server. A car's travel on highway with tollbooths is a representative metaphor of a request served in hardware servers.

1.2. KEY PERFORMANCE INDICATOR— TRANSACTION TIME

The users interact with the application by sending requests to execute particular business functions, for example:

- Generate a report on the sales of computers in the northeast region of the United States in the year 2000
- Consolidate financial data on bonuses paid to employees in the first quarter of the current year
- Load into the database data on all the items sold in January across company stores in New York State

A user's request forces the application to perform a particular amount of work to generate a response. This unit of work comprises the transaction; the time needed to complete the work is called *transaction response time* or *transaction time*. Transaction time is the most important characteristic of system performance from the user's perspective. If the users feel comfortable with the application's agility to process requests, then no additional efforts have to be made to speed up the application, no matter how long transaction times are. The acceptability of a transaction time by a business deviates greatly because it depends solely on the business users' conscious and unconscious anticipation of system agility. Business users in general have a fairly objective stance on transaction time. For example, they expect to get a reply in a matter of seconds when requesting the number of company stores located in New York City but are still pretty comfortable with more than a 1-minute processing of their request on the number of DVD players of different models sold in all the New York stores in January–March of the current year. The difference between two transactions is that the first one returns a number saved in a database, while the second one is actually an ad hoc request requiring analytical calculations on the fly.

On the other hand, if the system appears to the users to be slow and getting even slower and slower as more users log in, then the performance analyst has to use the tools of his trade to fix the issues. Application sizing and the tuning goal is to create an illusion for each user that he/she is the only person working with a system no matter how many other users are actively interacting with the application.

Application performance can be qualified as satisfactory or not only by the application's users; there is no formal metric to make such a distinction. If the users are comfortable with transaction times no efforts should be wasted to improve them (as a quest for the best usually turns out an enemy of the good because of the associated cost).

Applications can slow down not only when the number of active users increases, but also, in some instances, when additional data are loaded into database. Data load is a routine activity for enterprise applications, and it is scheduled to happen over particular time intervals. Depending on the application specifics and a company's logistics, a data load might be carried out every hour, every business day, once per week, once per month, or a data load schedule can be flexible. In several cases, loading new data makes the database larger and information processing more complex; all that has an impact on transaction times. For example, a transaction generating a report on sales volume in the current month might take an acceptable time for the first 10 days of the month, but after that it will take longer and longer with every following day if the data load occurs nightly.

Transaction time degradation can happen not only when the number of users or volume of data exceeds some thresholds, but also after the application is up and running for a particular period. A period can be as short as hours or as long as days or weeks. That is an indication that some system resources are not released after transactions are completed and there is a scarcity of remaining resources to allocate to new transactions. This phenomenon is called "resource leak" and usually has its roots in programming defects.

The natural growth of a business leads to an increase in rate (intensity) of requests from users as well as in data volume and data complexity; this makes periodic performance tuning and sizing an integral and mandatory part of the application life cycle.

Indicators of performance problems:

✓ Transaction response time is getting longer as more users are actively working with the system

✓ Transaction response time is getting longer as more data are loaded into system databases

✓ Transaction response time is getting longer over time even for the same number of users or data volume; that is a sign of "resource leak"

1.3. WHAT IS APPLICATION TUNING AND SIZING?

Application tuning is a course of action aimed at finding and fixing the bottlenecks in deployed systems for a given workload, data volume, and system architecture.

Application sizing takes place for planned applications as well as for existing production applications when they have to be scaled to accommodate a growth in the number of users and volume of data. Sizing delivers estimates of hardware architecture that ensures the quality of the requested service under an anticipated workload.

The sizing of the planned-for deployment systems as well as the tuning of the deployed systems are actually processes of removing limiting boundaries. There are two kinds of limits in enterprise applications:

1. Hardware limits: number of servers, number of CPUs per server, CPU speed, I/O speed, network bandwidth, and similar specifications of other hardware components

2. Software limits: parameter settings that define "throughput" of the logical "pipelines" inside the application (for example, number of threads, number of database connections, number of Web server connections, Java virtual machine memory size, etc.)

Performance engineering is the profession and obsession of improving an application's agility and users' satisfaction by removing software and hardware limitations; by removing boundaries it maximizes system throughput in a very cost-effective way. System tuning and sizing can be compared to processing plant optimization when different means and tools are applied in concert to increase a plant's output.

The complexity of enterprise applications makes their capacity planning and tuning projects effortful and demanding and even more so when they have to be executed in a limited time. Queuing network models clarify and interpret happenings in applications, framing their performance troubleshooting and sizing as logically organized processes that can be interpreted formally and therefore carried out successfully and efficiently.

1.4. QUEUING MODELS OF ENTERPRISE APPLICATION

In dealing with such intricate objects as enterprise applications we have to see the forest, not the trees. That is exactly what models help us to do: they shield our brains from numerous nonimportant and distracting details and allow us to concentrate on the fundamental processes in applications.

Models are capable of factoring in system architecture, the intensity of users' requests, processing times on different servers, as well as the parameters of hardware and a user's workload that are meaningful for performance analysis. Models also can assess the effects and the limitations of software parameters such as the number of threads, size of memory, connections to system resources, etc. At the same time models help to abstract from application specifics that might be substantial from a functionality perspective but irrelevant to sizing and tuning.

Why we are going to use **queuing** models to understand and solve application performance puzzles? The answer is that any system that provides services to the users has the users' requests waiting in queues if the speed of a service is slower than the rate of incoming requests. Consider a grocery store: people are waiting for checkout during peak hours. Another example: have you ever heard while dialing a bank: "All agents are busy serving other customers, please stay on the line and someone will answer your call in the order it was received"? In that case your call is put in a queue. If there is no waiting space in a queue you might hear: "All lines are busy now, try again later."

A few examples of the systems that can be presented by queuing models:

1. Bridge toll. Cars are requests; booths are servers.
2. Grocery store. Visitors are requests; counters are servers.
3. Cellular phone network. Phone calls are requests; phone towers are servers.
4. Internet. Click on a link initiates a request; networks and computers are servers.

Enterprise applications, like other systems serving multiple concurrent requests, have to manage different queues; they put incoming requests into waiting queues if particular services are busy processing previous requests. To size and tune applications we have to understand why queues are building up and find out how to minimize them. Queuing models are time-proven logical abstractions of real systems, and they clarify causes and consequences of queues on performance of multiuser systems [1.2, 1.3, 1.4]. Queuing models help us to understand event and processes relevant for sizing and tuning of computer systems: competition for resources among concurrent requests (CPU, memory, I/O, software threads, database connections, etc.) waiting in queues when resources are not available, the impact of the waits on transaction response times, and so on.

Queuing models represent applications by employing two constructs: transactions and nodes. A user's request initiates a transaction that navigates across a network of nodes and spends some time in each node receiving a service. Various publications on queuing models do not distinguish between the terms "request" and "transaction," assuming they mean the same thing. In such a case, the previous sentence can be rephrased: "A request navigates across a network of nodes and spends some time in each node receiving a service." We predominantly differentiate the two terms, but when we talk about queuing systems and queuing networks as mathematical objects, but not as application models, we use term "request" (this mostly relates to Chapter 2).

In this book we are dealing with two types of nodes. One type consists of two entities: queue and processing units (Fig. 1.5a).

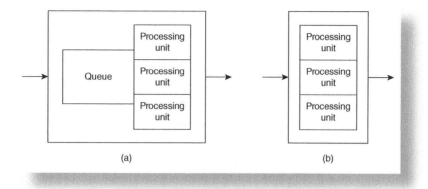

Figure 1.5. (a) A node with queue and processing units; (b) a node with processing units.

Processing units serve incoming transactions; if they are all busy, transactions will wait in the node's queue. The second type does not have a waiting queue but only processing units (Fig. 1.5b).

With a little imagination we can envision a transaction initiated by a user as a physical object visiting different hardware servers. A symbolic metaphor for a transaction is its representation as a car traveling on a highway with tollbooths. A tollbooth, in turn, is a metaphor for a hardware server.

Figure 1.6 depicts a relationship between an application and its queuing model. This is just one of many possible models of the same computer system; the model can represent a system on the different levels of abstraction. The model in Fig. 1.6 embodies system architecture; it has three nodes corresponding to the users, network, and hardware server.

Below are the relationships between the components of a real system and the components of its model:

Component of Application	Matching Component in Queuing Model
Users and their computers	Node "users"
Network	Node "network"
Server	Node "server"
Transactions initiated by users	Cars

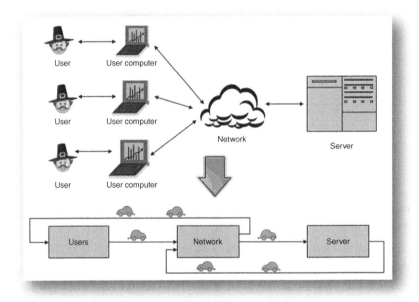

Figure 1.6.   An application and its queuing model.

A transaction starts its journey when a user clicks on a menu item or a link that implicitly initiates interaction with the application. In a model it means that a transaction leaves node "users" and is processed in the nodes "network" and "server." At the end of its journey, the transaction comes back to node "users." The total time a transaction has spent in the nodes "network" and "server" is the transaction time.

Transaction time is equal to the total time it has spent in all nodes except node "users."

A transaction (think of it as a car) coming into a node with a queue might either get served in a processing unit right away if there is at least one idle unit, or wait in a queue if all processing units are busy serving other requests (Fig. 1.7).

The total time spent by a transaction-car in a node with a queue is:

Time in queue + time in processing unit

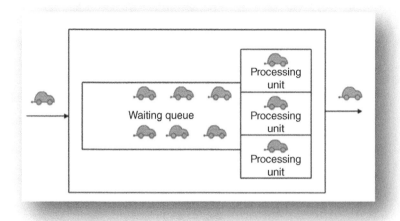

Figure 1.7.   Transactions in a node with waiting queue and processing units.

This simple formula demonstrates that time in queues has a major impact on transaction response time. If a transaction does not wait in any queues, then its response time is equal to the time it has spent in all processing units of all nodes it visited. That is always the case when only a single user is working. When many users are active, waiting in queues fundamentally influences system agility because the time in queues can be much longer than the processing time; as such, waiting in queues becomes the prevailing component of system response time. The number and speed of processing units, as well as the rate of incoming requests, are among the factors defining a node's queue length.

The nodes model different hardware components of the computer system; each component can be presented by a node on different levels of abstraction depending on the goal of the modeling project. For example, the following representation of a hardware server can be sufficient for the sizing of enterprise applications:

Hardware Server in Real System	Matching Object in Node
CPU	Processing unit
Number of CPUs	Number of processing units
CPU speed (computer clock speed)	Speed of processing unit

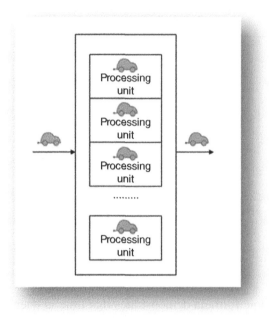

Figure 1.8.   A node as a network model.

Representation of a network by a node has to take into account network specifics. A network is a complex conglomerate of controllers, routers, bridges, and other devices interconnected by physical cables or wirelessly, and it can be portrayed by a model on different levels. For the sizing of enterprise applications, a corporate network can be modeled by a node without a queue but with an unlimited number of processing units (Fig. 1.8).

This network model takes into account the most important network parameter—network delay. Network delay for each transaction is equal to the time a transaction is served in a processing unit. Because of an unlimited number of processing units, the node does not have a waiting queue. The interpretation of a network by a node with unlimited processing units is an adequate representation of a corporate network because it always has enough capacity to start processing immediately every incoming transaction initiated by the corporation's users. We have to note, however, that this interpretation might not be suitable for networks with low bandwidth. For example, a network with dial-in connections can be represented by the node with a finite number of processing units equal to the number of connections and without queues. If an incoming transaction finds that all processing units are busy (which means all connections are already allocated), the incoming transaction will be rejected and a user will have to redial.

A node with unlimited processing units is also an adequate model of the users of the most common *interactive* enterprise applications. Consider how a user works with an *interactive* enterprise application (Fig. 1.6):

1. User initiates a transaction (car-transaction leaves node "users")
2. User waits for a reply (car-transaction is in nodes "network" or "server")
3. User receives a reply and analyzes it (car-transaction is in node "users")
4. User kicks off next transaction (car-transaction leaves a node "users")

The sequence of 1–4 depicts a process where the next transaction starts after a reply to the previous one is received by a user. This is the most common scenario for enterprise applications that usually are designed as *interactive* systems (http://en.wikipedia.org/wiki/Interactive) because they have to support execution of business task-flows broken down by a number of steps where each subsequent step depends on the results of the previous ones. A user implements each step by starting a transaction and will launch the next one only after analyzing the system's reply to the previous one. The interactive application's user interface prevents the user from submitting more than one request. Here is an example of a business taskflow "Update sales data for the North region":

- Login into the application
- Initiate the North region database
- Open the data input form for the North region
- Input new sales data and save the updated form
- Execute countrywide data consolidation to update country level sales because of new North region data

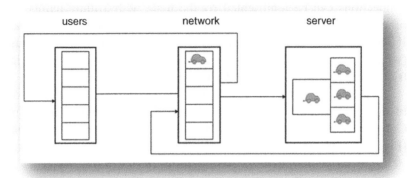

Figure 1.9.   Five transactions in both nodes "network" and "server."

- Run the financial report for country-level sales to make sure that data update for the North region was executed correctly
- Go to the next taskflow or log out

This example means that only one request per user is processed by an application at any given time. If a system has five users and all of them have launched transactions, then all five transactions (cars) will be served in the nodes representing the network and hardware server (Fig. 1.9).

The opposite situation occurs when all five users are analyzing data and are not waiting for the replies from system. In such a case, all five transactions are in node "users" and none are in the other two nodes (Fig. 1.10).

More often there is a situation when some users are waiting for replies and some users are analyzing results of completed previous transactions (Fig. 1.11).

From the examples of Figs. 1.9–1.11 we can conclude that in the queuing model of an *interactive* enterprise application, at any given time the number of transactions in all nodes are equal to the number of users who are logged into the system.

There are exceptions from the predominantly interactive nature of enterprise applications. Some applications allow particular business tasks to be executed in a noninteractive mode, letting users initiate a new transaction while waiting for completion of a previous one. This

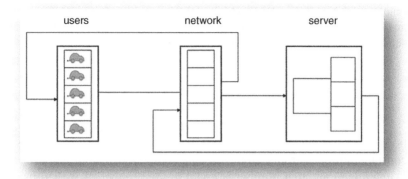

Figure 1.10.   Five transactions in node "users."

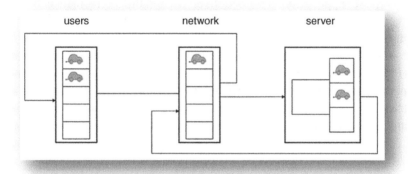

Figure 1.11.   Five transactions are distributed among the nodes.

case can also be modeled and here is how. Suppose the transaction "Financial consolidation for the North region" is long and takes dozens of minutes; after requesting it a user, instead of waiting for the reply, can demand the transaction "Financial consolidation for the South region." In such a case we take into consideration additional transactions by increasing the number of processing units in node "users." If we do that, the number of processing units in node "users" actually equals the number of transactions but no longer the number of users.

The finite number of users of enterprise applications represents one of their fundamental distinctions from Internet applications—the latter have practically an unlimited number of users.

Enterprise applications, in respect to number of users, are similar to shopping malls with hundreds and thousands of visitors, while Internet applications are similar to telephone networks with millions of users.

Because of the finite number of users, we model enterprise applications by the *closed* queuing model (Fig. 1.6), which always has a constant number of transactions moving from node to node; for *interactive* applications, that number is equal to the number of logged users. Actually, the quantity of logged users fluctuates during the workday and reaches a maximum during the hours of the most intense application usage. These hours are of utmost interest for analysis because the enterprise application has to deliver acceptable performance during such a critical period; it is advisable to evaluate models for the time of maximum application usage.

A model of Internet application is an *open* queuing network (Fig. 1.12) accepting requests from a user community that is permanently changing in size. In the open queuing model, the number of transactions at any given time can be anywhere in a range from "0" to any finite value.

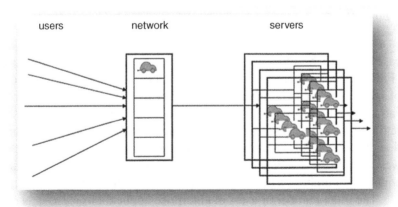

Figure 1.12.   Open queuing network as a model of an Internet application.

Mapping application into its queuing model

Application:	*Queuing network*
Server, hardware appliance, users, network:	*Node*
CPU, disk, I/O controller:	*Processing unit*
Transaction:	*Request (imagine a car)*
Waiting for system resource:	*Request in a waiting queue*

1.5. TRANSACTION RESPONSE TIME AND TRANSACTION PROFILE

What the users of enterprise applications care most about (as well as complain most about) is transaction response time. The user's final verdict on application performance is always based on the difference between the transaction time delivered by the application vs. the user's expectation of that time. Models provide great help in understanding the components of transaction time and the factors they depend on. Let's consider a business transaction that retrieves a financial report. The transaction is initiated when a user clicks on an icon labeled "Request Report." At that moment, let's start an imaginary stopwatch to measures transaction time. The initiated transaction [we again depict it as a car (see Fig. 1.13)] starts its journey by moving from one node to another, waiting in queues, and spending time in processing units. Finally the car-transaction will get back to the user, and we will stop the stopwatch at that moment. The time measured by the stopwatch is the transaction time—the sum of all time intervals a car-transaction has spent in waiting queues and processing units of all nodes that represent the system hardware. A "cloud" on Fig. 1.13 encompasses the nodes that contribute to transaction time. Transaction response time is the total of waiting and processing times in the nodes "network," "Web server," "Application server," and "Database server."

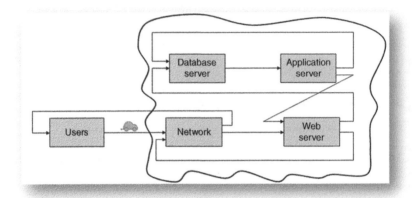

Figure 1.13.   Transaction time is time spent in the "cloud."

The table below describes the correlations among the happenings in an application and in its model:

Happenings in System	Happenings in Model
User initiated transaction by clicking on "Request Report" icon	Transaction entered cloud
Network serves transaction	Transaction served in node "network"
Transaction is processed in Web server	Transaction served in node "Web server"
Transaction is processed in Application server	Transaction served in node "Application server"
Processing in Application server requires data from the database; the Application server communicates a number of times with the database to retrieve data	Transaction served in nodes "Application server" and "Database server," visiting them a few times
After the financial report is finally generated by the Application server, the Web server processes the data to send them back over the network to a user	Transaction served in node "Web server"
Report travels back to a user over the network	Transaction served in node "network"
Now it is the user's time to analyze the report	Transaction served in node "users"

Figure 1.13 and the relationships described above indicate that transaction response time depends on the following factors:

- The number of active system users (users initiate requests; as more users initiate requests, there are more transactions in the nodes in a cloud, which means longer waiting queues)
- System architecture (more servers and connections among them allow for more varieties of transaction itineraries to exist in a cloud)
- The speed and numbers of the processing units in each node in a cloud
- Processing algorithms implemented in the application software

Transaction response time is a function of time intervals spent in the nodes that represent servers, networks, and other hardware components. It depends on the number of active users, hardware architecture, software algorithms, as well as the speed and number of hardware components.

The transaction profile is a set of time intervals a transaction has spent in all processing units (but not in queues!) it has visited while served by the application.

When analyzing applications' models we will need to know the **transaction profile**—the number of time intervals a transaction has spent in all processing units (but not queues!) it has visited while served by the application. Time in a particular processing unit is often called *service demand*.

This is an example of a transaction profile for a model on Fig. 1.13:

Transaction Name	Time Spent in Processing Units (Seconds)			
	Network	Web Server	Application Server	Database Server
Sales Report	0.05	0.5	3.2	1.0
Profit and Loss Report	0.03	0.8	4.2	2.0

By adding up times in the processing units visited by a single transaction while being served in a system, we have a transaction response time when only a single request was served by the application:

$$Sales\ report\ transaction\ time = 0.05 + 0.5 + 3.2 + 1.0 = 4.75\ seconds$$

$$Profit\ and\ Loss\ report\ transaction\ time = 0.03 + 0.8 + 4.2 + 2.0$$
$$= 7.03\ seconds$$

The above calculation is applicable for a transaction of a predominant type that is served sequentially in processing units. In some cases, a transaction's particulars allow its parallelization. There are two parallelization techniques that can be implemented by application software: (1) concurrent execution of the same transaction by a few hardware servers (for example, serving transactions in the application and database servers); and (2) concurrent execution of the same transaction by a few components of the same hardware server (for example, processing transactions by more than one CPU).

We demonstrate in Chapter 9 how to take parallelized transactions into account while modeling applications. In all other chapters we consider the prevailing types of transactions that receive services in processing units sequentially.

1.6. NETWORK OF HIGHWAYS AS AN ANALOGY OF THE QUEUING MODEL

We introduced the car-transaction metaphor previously. It helped to visualize how transactions travel along servers and networks, how they receive "treatment" in servers, and why they have to wait in the queues; it also clarified the meaning of transaction time and transaction profile. We want to "capitalize" on the car-transaction metaphor by making a parallel between the queuing model and a network of highways with tollbooths. That analogy helps performance engineers to illustrate some bottlenecks to nontechnical application business users.

Two things in my life consumed more time than anything else—sizing and tuning applications, and driving. The number of times I found myself stuck in heavy traffic while approaching a tollbooth made me think about the similarities between a queuing model's nodes and the tollbooths (Fig. 1.14).

A toll plaza usually has a few tollbooths that serve each car by taking payment. Payment processing requires some time, which is

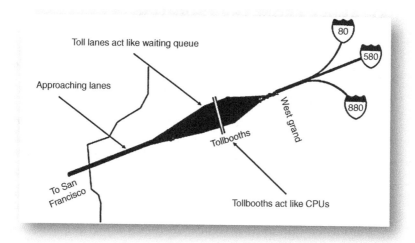

Figure 1.14.   Tollbooths as a node.

Figure 1.15.   Tollbooths with waiting queue and their model (source: http://www.hindu.com/2008/02/09/stories/2008020957590400.htm).

equivalent to time in a processing unit of a node. If all the tollbooths are busy, cars congregate on the approaching lanes of a toll plaza forming waiting queues—exactly like waiting queues in the nodes of queuing models (Fig. 1.15).

Now picture a car traveling from point A to point B and passing through a few tollbooths along the way; this is just like a transaction traveling across a queuing network. We are going to use the highway analogy of a queuing network when we feel that it provides an additional boost to imagination.

TAKE AWAY FROM THE CHAPTER

- *Closed queuing networks with a finite number of requests are representative models of enterprise applications, revealing causes of the bottlenecks and pointing to the right actions to troubleshoot them.*

- *A queuing model's nodes correspond to hardware servers, networks, and users; a node's processing units stand for CPUs; business transactions are characterized by the requests waiting and those being served in the model's nodes.*

- *The most important indicator of a business application's performance is transaction time; it depends on all time intervals a transaction has spent in system servers waiting in queues and being processed. A critical component of transaction time is its wait time in system queues; wait time is a function of the intricate interdependencies of multiple factors: hardware speed, number of users, intensity of a user's transactions, system architecture, settings of software parameters . . . the list goes on and on.*

- *A network of highways is a helpful analogy of queuing models when performance engineers communicate to nontechnical application business users.*

## CHAPTER 2

Building and Solving Application Models

In this chapter: the step-by-step process of model building; essentials of queuing theory; how to solve models and interpret modeling results.

2.1. BUILDING MODELS

In order to analyze performance of an enterprise application we have to create its queuing network model and study the model's output for various input data. This process includes:

- Specification of the hardware infrastructure hosting application
- Mapping the application into the model
- Definition of the model's input data
- Solving the model
- Calibrating the model
- Analyzing the output data for different "what-if" scenarios

We examine all the steps by considering a simple but representative application deployment on two Windows servers—one hosts a Web

Solving Enterprise Applications Performance Puzzles: Queuing Models to the Rescue,
First Edition. Leonid Grinshpan.
© 2012 Institute of Electrical and Electronics Engineers. Published 2012 by John Wiley
& Sons, Inc.

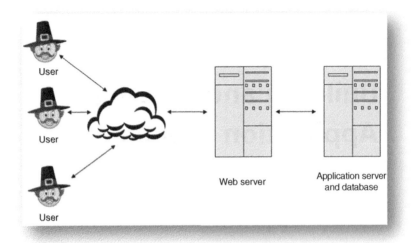

Figure 2.1. Two-server system.

server and the second one hosts both the application server and the database (Fig. 2.1); for convenience we will call the latter one the A&D server.

Hardware Specification

Specifications of the hardware servers in Windows 32-bit and 64-bit environments can be found by running a program *msinfo32.exe*, which is initiated by navigating *Start > All Programs > Run > msinfo32.exe*.

Figure 2.2 shows the hardware specifications of a Web server reported by utility *msinfo32.exe*.

The Web server has four CPUs, 3.6 MHz, 2 GB RAM; it is manufactured by IBM under the name "eserver xSeries 366." That information is needed to identify relative server performance based on benchmarks published either by IBM or by independent third parties. The hardware of the A&D server is specified in Fig. 2.3.

The A&D server has eight CPUs, 3.7 MHz, 3.7 GB RAM, and it is also manufactured by IBM under the name "eserver xSeries 366."

Finding the specifications of UNIX servers requires running different configuration commands depending on UNIX flavor and system manufacturer. For example, some Sun Solaris configuration commands are:

Item	Value
OS Manufacturer	Microsoft Corporation
System Name	PEW204
System Manufacturer	IBM
System Model	eserver xSeries 336 -[8837XX9]-
System Type	X86-based PC
Processor	x86 Family 15 Model 4 Stepping 1 GenuineIntel ~3600 Mhz
Processor	x86 Family 15 Model 4 Stepping 1 GenuineIntel ~3600 Mhz
Processor	x86 Family 15 Model 4 Stepping 1 GenuineIntel ~3600 Mhz
Processor	x86 Family 15 Model 4 Stepping 1 GenuineIntel ~3600 Mhz
BIOS Version/Date	IBM -[APE125AUS-1.08]-, 3/14/2005
SMBIOS Version	2.3
Windows Directory	C:\WINDOWS
System Directory	C:\WINDOWS\system32
Boot Device	\Device\HarddiskVolume1
Locale	United States
Hardware Abstraction Layer	Version = "5.2.3790.3959 (srv03_sp2_rtm.070216-1710)"
User Name	PEW204\Administrator
Time Zone	Eastern Standard Time
Total Physical Memory	2,047.31 MB
Available Physical Memory	1.02 GB

Figure 2.2. Specifications of the Web server.

- *psrinfo*: returns the number of CPUs
- *prtconfig*: returns RAM size
- *iostat*: returns I/O system configuration

The configuration commands for the operating systems AIX, HP-UX, Linux, and the others are usually described in system documentation available on the Internet. If you do not know a command name, do a search in www.google.com or www.bing.com for "AIX commands" or other UNIX flavors—you will be surprised by the richness of available information. Finding sufficient for modeling configuration data of UNIX servers might require execution of not just one but a few commands with properly defined parameters.

Operating system configuration commands and utilities provide information on hardware specifications needed for identification of a server's relative performance using benchmarking data.

Item	Value
OS Name	Microsoft(R) Windows(R) Server 2003, Enterprise Edition
Version	5.2.3790 Service Pack 2 Build 3790
Other OS Description	Not Available
OS Manufacturer	Microsoft Corporation
System Name	PEW205
System Manufacturer	IBM
System Model	eserver xSeries 366-[8863XX1]-
System Type	X86-based PC
Processor	x86 Family 15 Model 4 Stepping 1 GenuineIntel ~3669 Mhz
Processor	x86 Family 15 Model 4 Stepping 1 GenuineIntel ~3669 Mhz
Processor	x86 Family 15 Model 4 Stepping 1 GenuineIntel ~3669 Mhz
Processor	x86 Family 15 Model 4 Stepping 1 GenuineIntel ~3669 Mhz
Processor	x86 Family 15 Model 4 Stepping 1 GenuineIntel ~3669 Mhz
Processor	x86 Family 15 Model 4 Stepping 1 GenuineIntel ~3669 Mhz
Processor	x86 Family 15 Model 4 Stepping 1 GenuineIntel ~3669 Mhz
Processor	x86 Family 15 Model 4 Stepping 1 GenuineIntel ~3669 Mhz
BIOS Version/Date	IBM -[ZUE147BUS-1.08]-, 1/30/2006
SMBIOS Version	2.3
Windows Directory	C:\WINDOWS
System Directory	C:\WINDOWS\system32
Boot Device	\Device\HarddiskVolume1
Locale	United States
Hardware Abstraction Layer	Version = "5.2.3790.3959 (srv03_sp2_rtm.070216-1710)"
User Name	Not Available
Time Zone	Eastern Standard Time
Total Physical Memory	3,711.04 MB
Available Physical Memory	1.97 GB

Figure 2.3. Specifications of the A&D server.

Model Topology

A model topology is a combination of the nodes and the connections among them; in mathematical terms it is a graph: application users, networks, and hardware servers are represented by the nodes; connections between nodes depict transaction paths in the application (Fig. 2.4).

We mapped the system into a queuing model with three nodes: the nodes "Web server" and "A&D server" have processing units and waiting queues; the node "Users" has only processing units. The transactions initiated by the users travel to "Web server," after that they are processed by "A&D server" and return to node "Users" (transactions are represented by sedans in Fig. 2.4). The total transaction response time includes processing and waiting times in nodes "Web server" and "A&D server."

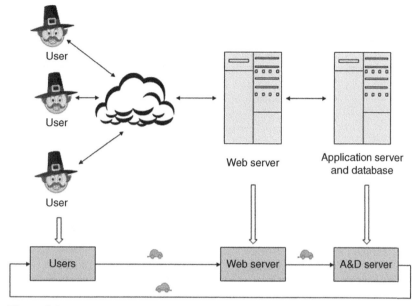

Figure 2.4. Queuing model of a two-server system.

A Model's Input Data

One of the most important steps in model building is specification of the model's input data. The success or failure of a modeling project is, to a large extent, defined by input data quality. Input data contains workload characterization and transaction profiles. Workload characterization consists of three components:

- List of business transactions
- For each transaction, the number of its executions at a particular time interval, usually during 1 hour (that number is called the transaction rate)
- For each transaction, the number of users requesting it.

The transaction profile is a set of time intervals a transaction has spent in all processing units it has visited while served by the application. For our example in Fig. 2.1, supported business transactions and their times for a single user are listed in Table 2.1.

Table 2.1
Transaction List and Times

	Transaction Name	Transaction Time for Single User
1	Logon	1.2 sec
2	Open application	1.1 sec
3	Logoff	0.2 sec
4	Consolidate	10.3 sec
5	Load file	3.1 sec
6	Force calculate	3.8 sec
7	Process control	0.5 sec
8	Set point of view (POV)	0.7 sec
9	Select entity	0.8 sec
10	Select parent	0.8 sec
11	Go to tasks menu	0.3 sec

The enterprise applications have a large nomenclature of transactions, but for performance analysis and modeling, we can reduce their number by excluding infrequently executed ones as well as by consolidating transactions we do not need to analyze individually. With that in mind the transactions listed in Table 2.1 can be broken down into three groups:

Group 1. Transactions 1 to 3 are executed only once every few hours or even once per workday—they can be excluded from the model's workload as their demand for the system resources is negligible.

Group 2. Transactions 7 to 11 represent service functions; as they do not implement business operations we do not need our model to provide their response times. Still, a demand from transactions 7–11 for system resources can be significant; in order to take it into account and at the same time to simplify the model we will consolidate transactions 7–11 into the one named "Navigation." The time of one "Navigation" transaction initiated by single users is 3.1 sec, and it is equal to the total time of the transactions 7–11.

Group 3. Finally we have a list of transactions for modeling (Table 2.2).

Table 2.2
List of Transactions for Model

	Transaction Name	Transaction Time for Single User
1	Consolidate	10.3 sec
2	Load file	3.1 sec
3	Force calculate	3.8 sec
4	Navigate	3.1 sec

The broad nomenclature of enterprise application transactions can be reduced without sacrificing workload accuracy by excluding some transactions and consolidating others.

Obtaining the transaction rate and profile might require substantial efforts including deployment of commercial transaction monitors (Chapter 3 elaborates on that). In simple cases, we can find a transaction profile by setting up monitoring utilities that are built into operating systems. The utilities record CPU utilization for each system server while manually executing a transaction multiple times. Suppose we carried out a described experiment for a system on Fig. 2.1 for transaction "Consolidate." We recorded an average transaction time of 10.3 sec; 10% of that time the Web server's CPU was utilized, and 90% of that time the A&D server's CPU was utilized. Assuming our transaction does not need I/O processing, we can conclude that transaction "Consolidate" spent 1% of its total time on the Web server (1.03 sec) and 90% of its total time on the A&D server (9.27 sec). Our experiment can be enhanced if we have access to a software load generator that can produce a steady sequence of transaction requests from a single virtual user. The system has to be exposed to a load for a period of time sufficient to collect statistically representative sets of transaction times and CPU utilizations.

Model Calibration

A calibrated model generates output data (transaction response times, server utilizations, etc.) close to the ones observed in a real production system. In order to calibrate a model we have to have at our disposal measurements of transaction response times as well as server utilizations collected on a production system for different numbers of users. We compare them with the model's output; in case of unacceptable discrepancies we must reevaluate the model's input data and recalculate the model.

Data for model calibration can be collected on a production system exposed to a load from real users. Unfortunately, the real workloads typically are very fluid and difficult to be "well defined"—they depend on many parameters that are not only out of our control but cannot even be measured with an acceptable degree of accuracy. Let's take for example the most important parameter of a workload—the number of users actively interacting with the system. In the enterprise environment the users are distributed across company offices located in different cities and even countries. It is very complicated to observe how many of the users who are logged in are active and how many just forgot to log out. As we do not know exactly the number of users we cannot discover transaction times and server utilization for a particular numbers of users.

All that means is that instead of desperate attempts to associate a real workload with transaction times and server utilization, we can expose the system to an artificial workload generated by software load generators. In such cases we are in full control over both the workload and the system, which ensures an acceptable correlation among workload, transaction time, and resources utilization.

Suppose that for the system in Fig. 2.1 we used a load generator and simulated a realistic workload from 10, 20, 60, and 80 users (Chart 2.1).

Chart 2.1 exhibits the special behavior of "Force Calculate" transaction: Its time starts growing exponentially when the number of users exceeds 30. Metrics on the servers' CPU utilization did not show that the capacity of any of them reached the saturation level (Chart 2.2).

We will learn later that this is an indication of a software bottleneck in our application. Analysis of the "Force Calculate" transaction functionality indicated that it generates new data and writes it into the database. Because of the substantial number of database locks that can happen for more than 30 users, "Force Calculate" requests have to wait until the locks are released, which increases response time. A calibrated model has to factor in the database locking effect.

The models of production systems have to be calibrated to ensure that they provide accurate output within calibration range.

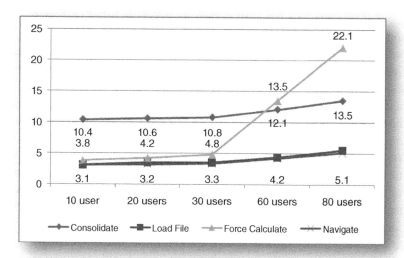

Chart 2.1.   Transaction times for different numbers of users.

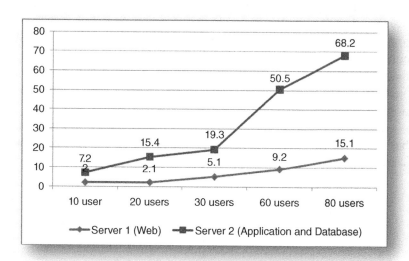

Chart 2.2.   Utilization of servers (%) for different numbers of users.

2.2. ESSENTIALS OF QUEUING NETWORKS THEORY

A significant contributor to the performance analyst's ability to deal with application performance puzzles is knowledge of the main concepts of the queuing network theory upon which all model analyzers are based. This section provides an introduction to queuing theory in order to facilitate the mastering of the book's subsequent material. Comprehension of the section does not require college-level mathematical knowledge; a familiarity with four arithmetical operations is sufficient. Readers who are interested in a more in-depth study of queuing theory application to computer system analysis are referred to *Quantitative System Performance. Computer System Analysis Using Queueing Network Models* by Lazowska et al. [2.1], which today is considered the definitive work on the modeling of computer systems (it is available for free download from http://www.cs.washington.edu/homes/lazowska/qsp/). In this book, we will use some notations and definitions from Lazowska et al. [2.1].

Queuing theory (as the name suggests) is the mathematical analysis of queues; because of its abstract nature it is applicable to many technical and social systems that feature waiting lines (enterprise applications are one of them). The theory has more than 100 years of history, starting from the paper by Danish engineer A.K. Erlang published in 1909; over the decades, the theory evolved into a rich discipline and proved to be indispensable for fundamental studies of various processes. We consider below a number of queuing theory results that show that the model's output data represent important performance characteristics of applications: utilization of servers, transaction times, number of transitions in waiting queues, etc.

The basic object of queuing theory is a node shown in Fig. 2.5; it has a waiting queue, a processing unit, and the flows of arriving and served requests.

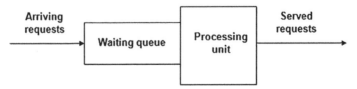

Figure 2.5.   A node with arriving and served requests.

Let's assume we observe the node during **I** sec and during that period **A** requests came into the system, **C** requests exited it (having been served), and the processing unit was busy **B** sec serving **C** requests. We can define the arrival rate as $\lambda = A/I$, node throughput as $X = C/I$, and the processing unit utilization as $U = B/I$. We also can find out that time **t** to serve one request in the processing unit is $t = B/C$ (**t** is service demand), and the processing unit is capable of serving $\mu = 1/t$ requests every second (μ is called the processing rate). Now we can find out the utilization of the processing unit depending on the node's throughput **X** and processing rate μ:

$$U = B/I = C/I * B/C = X * t = X/\mu.$$

If node throughput $X = \lambda$, which takes place when a number of arriving requests **A** is equal to a number of served requests **C**, then

$$U = \lambda/\mu.$$

An equation $X = \lambda$ (called the flow balance assumption [2.1]) is always satisfied in applications' closed queuing models, and we take it into consideration going forward.

In 1961, Professor John Little of the Massachusetts Institute of Technology published a remarkable formula that became known as Little's Law:

$$L = \lambda * W,$$

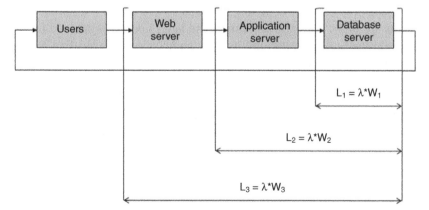

Figure 2.6. The number of transactions in different parts of the model per Little's law.

where **L** is the average number of requests in a node and **W** is the average time a single request spent in a node (in its queue and processing unit). The importance of the formula for queuing networks cannot be overestimated—it is applicable to any node inside a network, to any subset of nodes, as well as to the whole queuing network. That means, for example, that in the application model in Fig. 2.6 we can calculate the average number of transactions in the database only; in the database and application server; or in whole system, which includes Web, application, and database servers.

An important derivative from Little's law is the formula:

$$T = 1/(\mu - \lambda),$$

where **T** is the average time a request spends in a node's queue and processing unit [2.2]. That equation lets us find out the transaction response time in application models.

From Chapter 1 we know that enterprise applications are modeled by closed queuing networks. The latter are fully specified by the following input data:

- Number and type of each node
- Number **N** requests circulating in the network
- Service demand D_κ—time to serve request in a processing unit of node κ

Two types of nodes are sufficient to represent enterprise applications: the nodes with queues and the nodes without queues. A request arriving at the former node might be placed in a queue if all processing units are busy; a request arriving at the latter node will proceed immediately to the processing unit as their number is no fewer than **N**. The nodes with queues represent hardware servers, the nodes without queues model different kind of delays (for example, user think time).

A request arriving at a processing unit of a node κ spends time D_κ in it (we call it *service demand*). When a queuing network models an application, a set of service demands represents a transaction profile. Service demand time depends on numerous hardware and operating system parameters as well as software algorithms. For instance, service demand in a node modeling disk is a function of the speed of data transfer to and from the disk (write and read operations). In turn, for local disk a transfer rate is dictated by the disk rotation speed and seek time.

But if storage is connected over a fiber-optic line [as in case of a storage area network (SAN)], then the fiber-optic connection latency affects service demand. That means that models are capable of evaluating application performance depending on the technical specifications of hardware and software.

In real systems the satisfaction of a request might require multiple visits to a processing unit. For example, one I/O operation initiates 1,000 data reads from a disk, each taking 1 millisecond. An important characteristic of queuing networks is that their output data are the same for two representations of a service demand: either 1,000 visits to disk, each one demanding 1 millisecond, or one visit to disk demanding 1000*1 millisecond = 1 sec. That feature simplifies specification of the transaction profile.

Little's Law helps to overcome obstacles with model input data. Let's say we hit a roadblock trying to obtain a transaction profile for the model in Fig. 2.6: we can find its service demand for the database in a log file, but we cannot find or measure service demands for the Web or Application servers. All we can do is to calculate service demand for *both* the Web and Application servers by deducting from the total transaction time a service demand for the database. In such a case we have all input data for the model that has consolidated the Web and Application servers (Fig. 2.7).

Per Little's Law, the model will deliver representative output for total transaction time as well for all database parameters. That is sufficient, for instance, for evaluation of the impact of speed and the number of different database hardware servers on overall application performance.

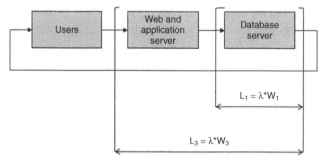

Figure 2.7.   Model with consolidated servers.

Table 2.3
Model's Output Data and Matching Performance Parameters
of Application

Model's Output Data	Matching Application Parameter
R—Average system response time	Average transaction response time
X—System throughput	Average number of transactions processed by application per second
U_κ—Utilization of node κ	Utilization of hardware server
R_κ—Average time a request spent in node κ	Average time transaction spent in a hardware server
X_κ—Node κ throughput	Average number of transactions processed by node κ per second
$Q\kappa$—Average number of requests in node κ	Average number of transactions in hardware server

After the input data are specified, a model can be solved and generate output data representing important application performance parameter. Table 2.3 lists the main model's outputs as well as examples of their associations with application performance indicators.

By solving models for a range of input data (for example, for different numbers of users) we can build charts that show the dependency of output performance parameters on changing input values. That makes possible analysis of different what-if scenarios needed for scientifically grounded decisions on application architecture.

Queuing networks can be analyzed using analytical as well as simulation methods.

An analytic technique to solve closed queuing models is based on a computational algorithm introduced by Jeffrey P. Buzen [2.3]. Closed model solvers use the mean value analysis (MVA) method developed by M. Reiser and S.S. Lavenberg [2.4]. The simulation approach employs computer imitation of a transaction processing in different nodes [2.5]. We will not go into details of the computational algorithm, MVA method, or simulation technology because manual use of any of them is suitable only for small models but not for the models of real multi-tier enterprise applications. For the latter we recommend using commercial "industrial strength" software packages; in some cases, open source programs can accomplish a task, although they require extra efforts to specify input data and interpret results. You will find an overview of the functionality of model solvers in the following paragraphs. For a synopsis of more than 40 leading tools being used in the field of performance analysis, modeling, and simulation please refer to Humayun, *An Overview of Some Network Modeling, Simulation, and Performance Analysis Tools* [2.6].

2.3. SOLVING MODELS

We demonstrate basic functionality of the model solver on the open source software package Java Modeling Tools (JMT) developed by Politecnico di Milano; it can be downloaded from http://jmt.sourceforge.net/. Let's start by defining input data for a model on Fig. 2.4.

The first thing we will notice in dealing with the modeling packages from different vendors is the diverse terminology. We have to pay attention to the definitions in order to interpret them correctly. In the JMT realm, a transaction is named "class" and the workload comprises a set of classes; each class has an assigned number of users. A workload of the model on Fig. 2.4 includes three transactions: "Report ABC" with 100 users; "Business Rule X" with 15 users, and "Consolidation Y" with 20 users. Because the number of users for each transaction in an enterprise application is constant we define each class as "closed." This is a definition of workload in JMT:

Next we define type of each node. JMT employs the term "station" for an object we have named a "node" in this book. A model for the system in Fig. 2.3 has three stations:

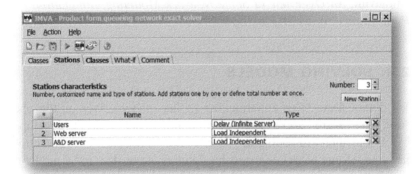

Station "Users" does not have queues as it has a number of processing units equal to the number of users ("Infinite Server" in JMT lingo). The stations "Web server" and "A&D server" are "load independent," which means the time to serve a request does not depend on the number requests waiting in a queue.

Next we have to input service demands for each transaction. As we noted, a set of the transaction's service demands depicts a transaction profile. That can be done by filling in a matrix that lists all the stations (nodes) and classes (transactions):

As you see, "Report ABC" is in node "Users" for 300 sec; it is processed by the "Web server" for 1 sec and by the "A&D server" for 8 sec. For transaction Business Rule X, service demands are 450 sec, 1.1 sec, and 25 sec in nodes "Users," "Web server," and "A&D server," respectively. Processing of a single Consolidation Y takes 1,200 sec in node "Users," 0.5 sec in "Web server," and 300 sec in "A&D server."

With all input data submitted, we can run the model's solving engine and get output information. Below is an example of data generated on that step. The "Utilization" tab provides "Web" and "A&D server" utilizations (the values have to be multiplied by 100 to have them expressed in percentages). What has to be noted is that the model provides not only aggregate node utilization, but how much each class (transaction) contributed to it. This has significant practical advantage as it helps to identify the most demanding application transactions. The utilization metric of the "Users" node in JMT is somewhat specific—it is given in an average number of users in the node. It can be easily calculated as a percentage because the total number of users is 135; for example, aggregate average utilization of the Users node is

$$(23.23/135) * 100\% = 17.2\%.$$

JMVA Solutions _ □ x

Throughput \ Queue length \ Residence Times \ Utilization \ Synopsis \

Utilization
Utilization of a customer class at the selected station. The utilization of a delay station is the average number of customers in the station (it may be greater than 1)

*	Aggregate	Report ABC	Business Rule X	Consolidation Y
-	-	-	-	-
Users	23.232640	9.627816	9.432199	4.172626
Web server	0.056888	0.032093	0.023056	0.001739
A&D server	0.685694	0.128371	0.209604	0.347719

The "Residence Times" tab displays the times spent by transactions in each node (including time in queues):

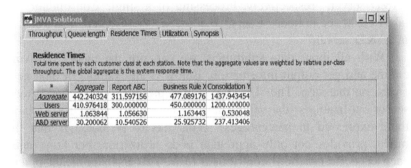

Total transaction time is a sum of the times it has spent in nodes "Web server" and "A&D server."

The JMT package enables analysis of what-if scenarios. For example, we can double the number of users in each class:

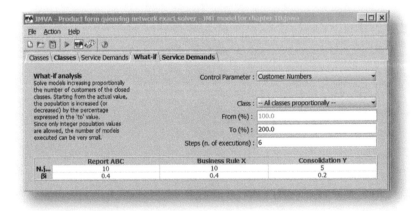

We also can modify the transaction profile by changing service demands. This is how to increase from 4 sec to 8 sec the time Report ABC spends on the A&D server.

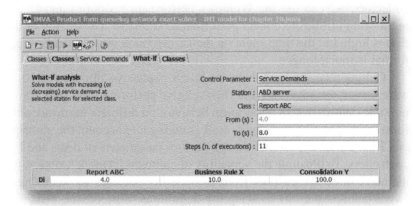

Demonstrated JMT functionality is provided by its analytical MVA component. JMT also includes a simulation engine [2.7] with the same capability.

JMT is a convenient tool for queuing network solving, but its potential is not sufficient for productive analysis of queuing models of enterprise applications. That limitation does not preclude us from using JMT to analyze complex models and diversified what-if scenarios. It just means we have to do additional work to transform specifications of real applications and its hosting hardware into strict input format that is understandable by JMT. Commercial software packages facilitate more dynamic and convenient model analysis as they accept input data in a form of hardware and software specifications and benchmarks; they also automate comparison of multiple what-if scenarios.

Commercial solvers typically are components of broader suites that, among other programs, include collectors of a model's input data. Collectors stand for software utilities deployed on hardware servers; they measure transaction profiles as well as extract information from system performance counters (CPU and I/O utilizations, memory consumption, queue lengths, numbers of read/write operations, threads, connections, etc.; the list goes on and on [2.8, 2.9]). Some model solvers also recognize input data gathered by popular IT management systems such as OpenView by Hewlett Packard (www.hp.com), Tivoli by IBM (www.ibm.com), or Vantage by Compuware (http://www. compuware.com). If we are deprived of the convenience of data collectors, we can use the Windows Performance Monitor and UNIX monitoring utilities to collect performance counters. The quality of the data is high, but the time spent on their conversion into a model's input format is much longer.

Commercial model solvers maintain expansive libraries of hardware server specifications and their relative performances. That makes possible comparison of application behavior on different hardware platforms and operating systems as well as taking into account the numbers of CPUs, cores, hyper-threads, and various parameters of disks and I/O controllers. To illustrate the versatility of commercial model solvers, we included three screenshots from a modeling package by TeamQuest (www.teamquest.com) showing the definitions of processor, disk, and I/O controller (Figs. 2.8, 2.9, and 2.10; screenshots are courtesy of

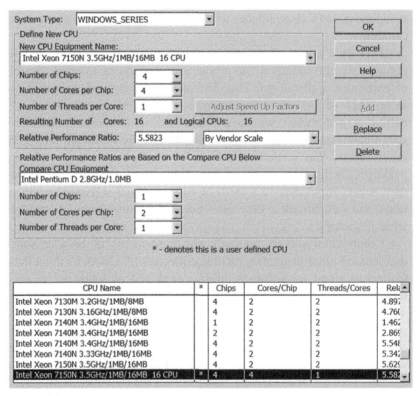

Figure 2.8. Definition of a processor includes CPU type, clock speed, number of chips, cores, threads, chip cache size, RAM size, and CPU relative performance.

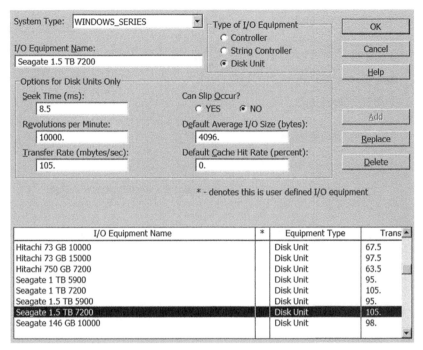

Figure 2.9. Definition of a disk includes seek time, number of revolutions, transfer rate, and average size of data per I/O operations.

TeamQuest Corporation). Each picture lists the hardware parameters a model factors in while calculating outputs; evidently all parameters are technical ones and well familiar to computer engineers.

The hardware libraries are opened to the users and can be populated with custom information describing user-specific hardware. A library's openness and expandability lets users adapt model solvers to their environments—a Herculean task for model vendors.

Rich solvers' libraries speed up comparison of different application deployment architectures—an activity any performance analyst has to carry out frequently to deliver service level requested by the business. Variations in hardware server configurations, specifications, as well as hosted operating systems are reflected in relative performance ratios (see Fig. 2.8). Using performance ratios, model solvers immediately recalculate service demand values for nodes affected by what-if scenarios and generate new output data.

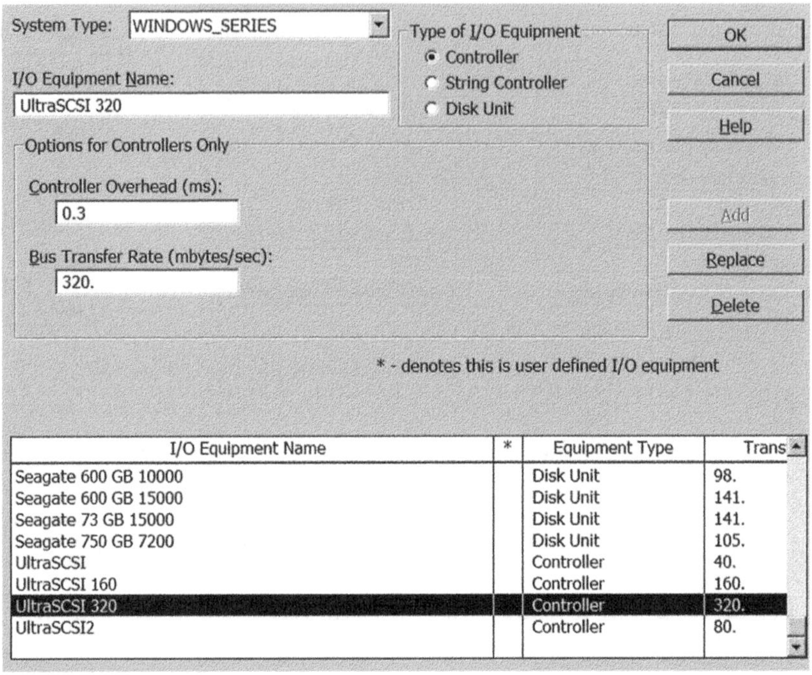

Figure 2.10. Definition of the I/O controller includes its overhead (time it serves I/O operation) and I/O bus speed.

Commercial packages are capable of modeling bottlenecks that are due to resource limitations (such as memory size, number of software threads and server connections, etc.). To use that functionality we have to define the total amount of available resources (for instance, 50 database connections) as well as the quantity allocated to one transaction (let's say the transaction Retrieve Profit & Loss Statement needs two database connections). Under a multiuser workload, all connections might be allocated, and some transactions will wait until connections are released; model solvers will factor in that wait time in the total transaction time.

Commercial model solvers speed up the modeling process in a number of ways to make performance analysts more productive. Here are a few of them:

- Accepting as an input a range of the number of users (for instance, 10, 50, 100, and 200), calculating results for all of them, and automatically building charts of output values as functions of a number of users

- Setting up new what-if scenarios—not from scratch but by modifying previous scenarios
- Keeping track of all the changes made along the modeling process and allowing for a performance analyst to go back and repeat the previous steps

A menu of such enhancements depends on the modeling package; descriptions of packages and their functionality may be found by visiting vendors' websites:

Vendor	Product	URL
TeamQuest	TeamQuest Model	http://teamquest.com/products/index.htm
BMC Software	ProactiveNet	http://www.bmc.com/products/product-listing/ProactiveNet-Performance-Management.html
Metron Technology	athene	http://www.metron-athene.com/athene/index.html
CA Technologies	HyPerformix	http://www.ca.com/us/capacity-management.aspx http://www.hyperformix.com/solutions/capacity-planning
OPNET	AppCapacity**Xpert**	http://www.opnet.com/solutions/brochures/AppCapacityXpert.pdf

2.4. INTERPRETATION OF MODELING RESULTS

Model solvers generate output data an analyst has to review in order to decide what actions to take to improve application performance. We discuss how to associate mathematically calculated modeling results with application performance indicators.

Hardware Utilization

When a transaction is processed by a hardware server it consumes its capacity. A server with only one CPU is fully utilized while working on a transaction; if the server has a few CPUs, then evaluation of its

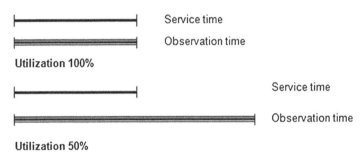

Figure 2.11. Service and observation times.

utilization requires slightly more elaborated logic. A utilization metric is vital since it lets IT departments ensure that expensive hardware provides the anticipated return on investment and at the same time it is capable of delivering the requested application's service level.

Models help recognize factors that affect hardware utilization. If we are looking at a processing unit only during the time when a transaction is served in it (we called it service demand time), we see that the unit is 100% busy. If we extend our observation interval beyond service demand time we will notice that for part of an observation interval a processing unit is 100% busy and at another point it is idle. Figure 2.11 illustrates relations between service and observation times.

The processing unit utilization depends on both service and observation times, and utilization is equal to the percentage of the observation time a unit was busy serving the transaction:

Utilization = (Service demand time/Observation time) * 100%

The observation time of operating system monitoring utilities is often called the "sampling interval." Monitoring utilities calculate CPU utilization at each sampling interval and present it as a percentage of time a CPU was busy during the sampling interval. Figure 2.12 captures the Windows Task Manager showing CPU utilization at 29%.

For practical and technical considerations, the preset sampling interval is usually in a range from 1 to 10 sec, but it can be changed. For example, it is the first parameter of the UNIX **vmstat** command,

Figure 2.12. CPU utilization reported by Windows Task Manager.

```
kthr       memory              page                    faults         cpu
----- --------------  -------------------------  --------------  -----------------
 r  b   avm    fre   re  pi  po  fr    sr  cy   in    sy   cs  us sy id wa
 1  0 22478  1677    0   0   0   0     0   0  188  1380  157  57 32  0 10
 1  0 22506  1609    0   0   0   0     0   0  214  1476  186  48 37  0 16
 0  0 22498  1582    0   0   0   0     0   0  248  1470  226  55 36  0  9
```

Figure 2.13. CPU utilization reported by the UNIX utility **vmstat**.

which provides performance statistics for different components including CPU utilization:

vmstat <length of sampling interval>

<number of sampling intervals>

We have to be aware that if we set a short sampling interval, it increases monitoring overhead but provides a more accurate metric; a long interval minimizes overhead, but it raises the chances of missing spikes in utilization that might be causing performance degradation.

CPU utilization reported by the **vmstat** command is shown in the circled data in Fig. 2.13.

As we have learned, queuing models calculate processing unit utilization using the formula:

$$U = \lambda/\mu,$$

where λ is the rate of arriving requests, and μ is the processing rate.

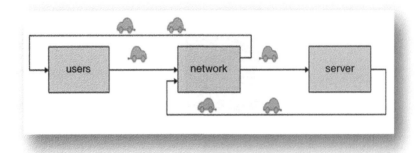

Figure 2.14.   Utilization of the node "server" is higher when nodes "users" and "network" are faster.

It is straightforward to conclude that a higher rate of arriving requests λ leads to higher node utilization and vice versa. Conversely, a higher processing rate μ leads to lower utilization.

This formula provides the same utilization values for the models as the monitoring tools for real systems. For that reason we can find out from models what impacts server utilizations in real systems.

Firstly, what does the rate of arriving requests depend on? One factor is easy to recognize: it is the number of users. More users mean more transactions are crisscrossing the queuing network and hitting each node more often. Identification of additional factors is equal to a small discovery—those are the **processing rates** in the other nodes of the model.

Take a look at the model in Fig. 2.14. Let's assume that each user represented by node "users" generates the next request immediately after the previous one came back to him. Let's also assume that network delay is almost nonexistent. In such a case a car-request will return to node "server" right after leaving it; that means we have a very high rate of requests entering node "server."

The model suggests that we have a higher rate of requests entering a particular node by speeding up processing in some other nodes (in real systems it happens, for example, by switching to a network with higher speed). Per the utilization formula, higher rates of arriving requests lead to higher node utilization.

We came to a nontrivial conclusion: If we increase the speed of a node to eliminate its bottleneck, the latter might move to another node.

Consider a real situation: An application is deployed on a server farm in a datacenter located in New York. When it is nighttime in the United States, the application is in use by 100 employees located in India, Australia, China, and Japan; average utilization of servers is 85%. During the day in the United States, only 70 U.S.-based employees are using the system. What seems unusual at first is that just 70 U.S. users load the system to 100%. The difference is due to higher network speed in the US—it delivers user requests to the server farm much faster than it does it for overseas users.

An increase in speed of any hardware component of a computer system might lead to higher utilization of some other components because of the higher rate of incoming requests. Does it sound like fixing a bottleneck on one server can move it to another?

For IT departments in charge of application maintenance, knowledge of the utilization of hardware servers for different numbers of users is critical. During spikes in workload, it helps to take preventive actions to avoid poor application performance or even downtime. For a period of low application usage, an IT department can reallocate hardware resources to other tasks if the application is hosted in a virtual environment.

In addition to total server utilization by workload, models deliver utilization of servers by each transaction. That parameter allows us to discover the most demanding transactions for each server. It is valuable information for application maintenance because the most demanding transactions are potentially the most disruptive ones and have to be monitored closely. When such transactions are identified by models, application administrators can grant access to a limited category of users for these transactions, for example, only to region managers.

Server Queue Length, Transaction Time, System Throughput

Server queue length is indicative of the size of memory allocated to waiting transactions; usually a server that has long waiting queues requires a larger RAM. A server's queue length impacts the time a transaction spends in it; the model calculates that time for each node, including the time in its queue. Based on that parameter it is possible to discover the server that adds the most to total transaction response time. A performance analyst can recommend to replace it with the faster one or to review the software algorithm.

Transaction time is the most important application parameter for business users. It is calculated by solvers for each transaction defined in the model's workload and represents an average value if the solver is based on the MVA method, or it might have minimum, average, and maximum values if the solver is based on simulation technology.

In the previous chapter we compared an application to a processing plant; in concert with that analogy, applications are characterized by a parameter called "throughput": it indicates the number of transactions an application processes for a given time interval under a specified workload and transaction profile. There is a slight conflict of interest between the business using the application and the IT department that maintains it. The former is concerned with an acceptable transaction time while the latter is interested in lowering hardware costs by increasing its usage and, by the same token, its throughput that potentially leads to higher transaction times. Such conflicts are occurring more often with the proliferation of virtual platforms, when IT shares the same physical environment among multiple applications by setting up virtual machines. A model is a convenient moderator in that conflict because it provides all necessary data, including throughput, to find a satisfactory solution for all sides.

We illustrate the connection between transaction time and system throughput on the simplest application model with only two nodes. The first one represents users and the second one, with eight processing units, is associated with a consolidated "Web," "Application," and "Database" server (Fig. 2.15).

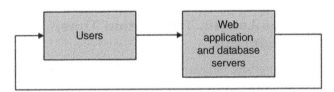

Figure 2.15. Model of three-tiered application hosted on one hardware server.

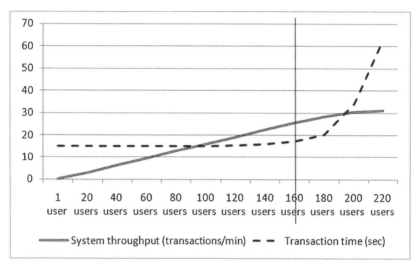

Chart 2.3. Correlation between transaction time and system throughput.

The model's input data: number of users is 20, 40 . . . 200, 220; service demand in node "Users" is 360 sec; service demand in nodes "Web," "Application," and "Database" servers is 15 sec; workload consists of one transaction. A model solver generated data for Chart 2.3; it can be seen that increasing the number of users above 160 leads to a transaction time exponential degradation and to a growth of throughput that maxes out at 32 transactions/min. Based on Chart 2.3, an analyst can recommend limiting the number of system users to 160; in such a case, transaction time is still acceptable to the business and system throughput is 17 transactions/min.

A curve representing the transaction time reminds us of a hockey stick because it has a sharp bend as the number of users grows. This is a reflection of a general feature of any enterprise application: when exceeding a certain number of users, its transaction time deteriorates considerably. Models are capable of forecasting the threshold value leading to the "hockey stick effect."

The correlation among number of users, transaction response time, server utilization, and queue length is illustrated on Chart 2.4. The model reveals that transaction time deterioration starts when the server node reaches 80–85% utilization, and it is accompanied by accelerated queue length growth.

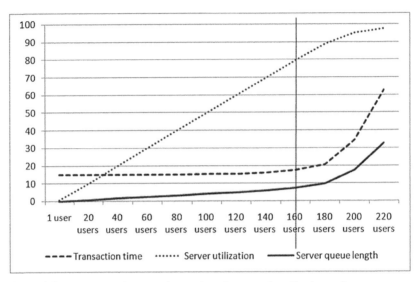

Chart 2.4. Correlation between the number of users and application performance.

The importance of obtained results goes far beyond this example, as it exhibits a general behavioral pattern of enterprise applications: There is a "breaking point" in the number of users an application can support without substantial degradation of transaction time. This point is reached when utilization of *any* hardware component (CPU, I/O subsystem, etc.) is 80–85%. The applicability of that result to *any* hardware component is based on Little's Law, which is valid for any node inside a network, for any subset of nodes, as well as for whole queuing network.

In the following chapters we harness the power of queuing network models to reproduce and analyze bottlenecks in enterprise applications and expose the causes of bottlenecks and their remediation.

TAKE AWAY FROM THE CHAPTER

- *To analyze performance of an enterprise application we have to create its queuing network model and study model's output for various input data. This process includes:*

- *Specification of the hardware infrastructure hosting the application*
- *Mapping the application into a model*
- *Definition of the model's input data*
- *Solving the model*
- *Calibrating the model*
- *Analyzing output data for different what-if scenarios*

- *Operating systems include utilities that report technical specifications of hardware servers as well the trade names that are needed to identify relative server performance based on benchmarks published either by vendors or by independent third parties.*

- *A model's input data contain workload characterization and transaction profiles. Workload characterization consists of three components:*
  - *List of business transactions*
  - *Per each transaction, the number of its executions at a particular time interval, usually during 1 hour (that number is called the transaction rate).*
  - *Per each transaction, the number of users requesting it.*

A transaction profile is a set of time intervals a transaction has spent in all processing units it has visited while served by the application.

- *To analyze models we can use commercial or open source model solvers. Commercial packages are preferable because of their versatility in making modeling more productive.*

- *Model solvers are based on fundamental results of queuing theory and implement either analytical or simulation algorithms. They generate output data that are essential for making decisions on application performance improvement. A model's outputs are representative estimates of application performance indicators (transaction times, system throughput, waiting times, queue lengths, etc.).*

- *Calibrated models generate output data close to the ones observed in a real production system. In order to calibrate a model, we collect production system measurements of transaction response times and server utilizations for different numbers of users and compare them with a model's output; in case of unacceptable discrepancies we must reevaluate the model's input data and recalculate the model.*

- *An increase in the speed of any hardware component of a computer system might lead to higher utilization of some other components because of the higher rate of incoming requests.*

- *There is a threshold in the number of users an application can support without substantial degradation of transaction time. This threshold is reached when utilization of any hardware component (CPU, I/O subsystem, etc.) is 80–85%.*

## CHAPTER 3

Workload Characterization and Transaction Profiling

In this chapter: application workload and its characterization; analysis of workload variations using "think time" and "garbage in, garbage out" models; number of application users and user concurrency model; business process analysis; how to uncover transactional data from production applications.

3.1. WHAT IS APPLICATION WORKLOAD?

Every tuning and sizing project has to begin from the characterization of the workload an application is intended to support at the service level requested by a business. The reason is obvious—tuning and sizing always are implemented for a particular workload even if we are not aware of their parameters (if that sounds surprising, then it is similar to a sudden discovery that in our ordinary life we speak in prose). If we do not know the workload specifications but we tuned or sized the application, then the application will perform at its best under the

Solving Enterprise Applications Performance Puzzles: Queuing Models to the Rescue, First Edition. Leonid Grinshpan.
© 2012 Institute of Electrical and Electronics Engineers. Published 2012 by John Wiley & Sons, Inc.

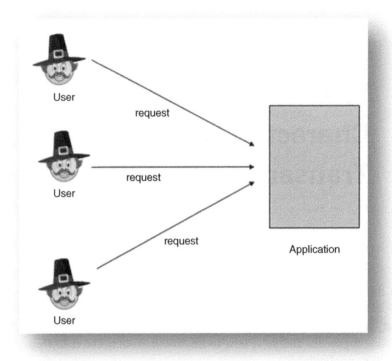

Figure 3.1. Application workload.

workload it was tuned or sized for. The problem is that the real production workload might be very different and, regretfully, our recommendations do not have practical value; moreover, they are misleading. A performance engineer has to pay the utmost attention to workload characterization, which is the cornerstone of every successful tuning and sizing project.

A general concept of a system workload is elusive, and there is no commonly accepted definition [3.1]. We are in a much better position because within the context of this book we are interested only in the more specific **application workload**. In the realm of enterprise applications there are two interacting entities: the application and its users (Fig. 3.1).

The users submit requests to the application to execute particular tasks; the application processes information to satisfy them and sends replies back to the users. Interactions between user and application are called transactions. **We define application workload as a flow of**

transactions initiated by users forcing the application to do some amount of work in order to generate the replies.

Application workload is a flow of transactions initiated by users that an application has to process.

The amount of work fluctuates significantly depending on the intensity of a user's requests. If the workload is higher than the application's capacity to process it efficiently, response time will grow because the queues will build up in the system. If the workload is light and underutilizes hardware capacity, then the system is apparently too expensive and provides low return on the money spent on its purchase, deployment, and maintenance. An application, in respect to workload, can be compared to an oil refinery: a refinery processes crude oil using available machinery; a balance between the incoming flow of crude oil and the plant's capacity makes the plant cost-effective. To make an application that is cost-effective and performs well, we have to achieve a balance between workload and system capacity. We do this by tuning and sizing the application.

Enterprise applications have a very rich functionality with heterogeneous workloads consisting of a variety of requests to implement different business tasks. The tasks differ in the amount of time and system capacity they consume for processing. Workload is characterized by transactions and their rates (intensity); the rates are measured in the number of transactions coming to the application from the users during a particular time interval (for example, if the interval is 1 hour, the transaction rate is measured in transactions/hour). A well-characterized workload is a prerequisite that enables correct executions of the tuning and sizing projects.

The values of an application's tuning parameters, as well as estimates of its architecture delivered by capacity planning, depend on workload; tuning and sizing parameters of the same application exposed to different workloads are different. That means there is no such thing as an optimally sized and tuned application no matter what workload is generated by its users. If that were the case, then the performance engineering body of knowledge would consists of a few rules written in stone: just follow them and an application that perfectly performs in all circumstances is delivered!

Tuning parameters and sizing estimates of the same application that is exposed to different workloads are different.

As an example, let's consider an application that has only one hardware server hosting all software components. A performance evaluation of such an application might conclude that in order to provide acceptable service under a workload with an intensity of 500 transactions/hour, a server's Java virtual machine (JVM) has to have a maximum heap size of 256 MB; for a workload with 1,500 transactions/hour, the JVM has to have a maximum heap size of 1 GB. Setting the JVM maximum heap size at 1 GB will degrade system performance for a workload equal to 500 transactions/hour because of the longer time a garbage collector will take to clean up JVM memory.

To emphasize the importance of workload specification, let's refer to our analogy between an application's model and a network of highways. When construction engineers are charged with fixing bottlenecks on a toll plaza, the first thing they will do is to analyze the traffic pattern and measure its specifications. Engineers will provide recommendations on the number of additional tollbooths as well as the number of approaching lanes only based on the traffic statistics. We would live in a more efficient world if all performance tuning and sizing projects were executed in a similar way: workload analysis first and tuning and sizing to follow.

3.2. WORKLOAD CHARACTERIZATION

Workload characterization for tuning and sizing includes:

- A list of business transactions
- The rate of each business transaction—the number of its executions per 1 hour per requests from one user
- The number of users requesting each business transaction

Workload specifies a blend and a rate of transactions generated by application users during a particular time interval.

This is an example of workload characterization:

List of Business Transactions	Number of Users Initiating Transaction	Transaction Rate (Average Number of Transactions Initiated by One User for 1 Hour)
Retrieve financial report	100	5
Consolidate sales data	25	2
Post number of parts sold	400	2

It definitely does not look frightening—we do not need to hunt for exotic data to quantify the workload. We can either retrieve statistical metrics from the production system or interview application business users if we intend to do capacity planning. Workload characterization also can be found in a service level agreement (SLA), which is a comprehensive document specifying services and their quality that the business expects to be provided by an application to its users. In the application life cycle, the SLA is supposed to be written and agreed upon before application deployment. It is a gold mine filled with a model's input data.

The ways to simulate characterized workloads are different for sizing and tuning projects. When we build a model for application sizing we substitute a planned system and its users with a model; to solve the model we have to quantify a flow of transactions (Fig. 3.2).

For systems tuning we usually employ special software to emulate the activities of real users; this software is often called load generators [3.2, 3.3, 3.4, 3.5]. Load generators provide a flexible and controlled environment for tuning. For any tuning project we have to ensure that a load generator submits the same mix and rate of requests as real users would do (Fig. 3.3).

Transaction Rate and User Think Time

The average number of the same transaction initiated by one user for 1 hour is a characterization of the rate of requests generated by a user. The customary activity of a user of an interactive application consists of sending a request, getting a reply, analyzing it, sending the next request, and repeating that sequence over and over again during a few hours or a workday. User activity is pictured in Fig. 3.4. It can be seen

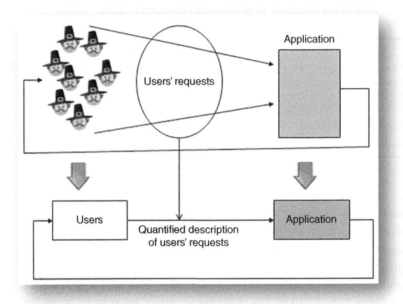

Figure 3.2. Model of planned application.

that the user think time (the period when the user analyzes a reply from the application and prepares a new request) is substantial and in many cases it takes a major part of the cycle of user–application interaction. User think time impacts the intensity of requests an application has to process and the utilizations of system servers also depends on it.

Average user think time is calculated per this formula:

$$Average\ user\ think\ time\ (seconds) = \frac{3600\ seconds}{average\ number\ of\ transactions\ initiated\ by\ one\ user\ per\ one\ hour}$$

The transaction rate generated by one user is defined either by a user think time or by the number of transactions for one user for 1 hour. Both metrics are equal; which one to use is only a matter of convenience and depends on the format required by the modeling or load generation tool employed for a project.

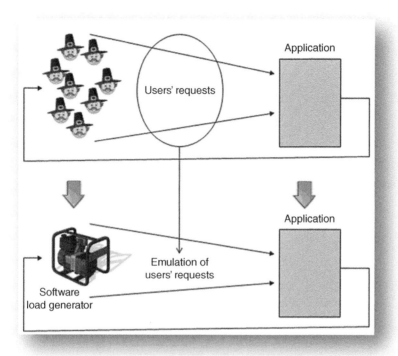

Figure 3.3. Substitution of users by a software load generator for application tuning.

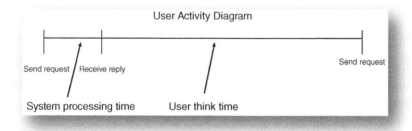

Figure 3.4. User think time.

User think time is represented in an application's models by a processing time in the node "users." Let's take a look at a model in Fig. 3.5. It has two nodes—"Users" and "Server," as we assume that all software components of an application are hosted on one computer.

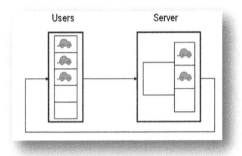

Figure 3.5. Application model with two service nodes and nonzero think time.

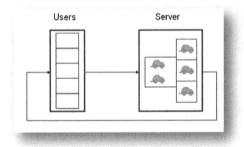

Figure 3.6. Application model with two service nodes and zero think time.

The model represents an interactive application with five users. The location of cars-transactions on the picture suggests that two transactions are currently being processed by the application, which means two users are expecting their replies to come back. The remaining three users did not initiate any transactions, and they are in a "user think time" mode.

To demonstrate the importance of user think time, we consider two hypothetical marginal situations. If we assume that user think time is zero, then all five transactions always will congregate in the "Server" node; three of them will be in processing units and two will be in a waiting queue (Fig. 3.6); that means the "Server" node will be utilized 100%. If we assume the opposite—that user think time is indefinite—then the node "Server" is always going to be idle (Fig. 3.7).

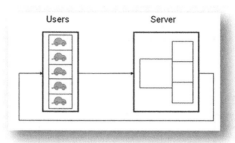

Figure 3.7. Application model with two service nodes and indefinite think time.

Table 3.1
Workload and Transaction Profile for the Model "Think Time"

Workload			Transaction Profile
Transaction Name	Number of Users	Time in Node "Users"	Time in Node "Server"
Transaction A	5 and 10	360, 36, 3.6, and 0.36 sec	7 sec

Think Time Model

To analyze the impact of think time on transaction time we solve the model in Fig. 3.5 for a few think time values: 360 sec, 36 sec, 3.6 sec, and 0.36 sec; we also suppose that a server's processing unit takes 7 sec to process a single request before sending it back to a user.

The model's input data are described in Table 3.1.

For five users, the model predicts an increase in transaction time from 7 sec to 10 sec when think time changes from 360 sec to 0.36 sec (Chart 3.1).

The impact of think time on transaction time is much more pronounced if we have not 5 but 10 users (Chart 3.2); in that case, transaction time grows from 7 sec to 23 sec.

Think time value is also crucial for server utilization; decreasing it from 360 sec to 3.6 sec leads to server saturation (Chart 3.3, 10 users in system).

Think time is in inverse correlation with the number of transactions the system processes at any given time interval. A smaller think time

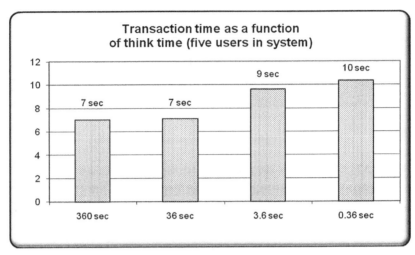

Chart 3.1. Transaction time as a function of think time (five users).

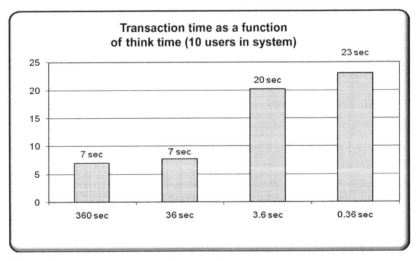

Chart 3.2. Transaction time as a function of think time (ten users).

leads to a higher transaction rate until the system reaches the limit of its capacity and the transaction rate flattens (Chart 3.4).

Charts 3.1–3.4 underscore how critical the impact of user think time and transaction rate are on application performance. Realistic values of both parameters ensure that sizing and tuning project deliverables are correct. Skewing the think time or transaction rate one way

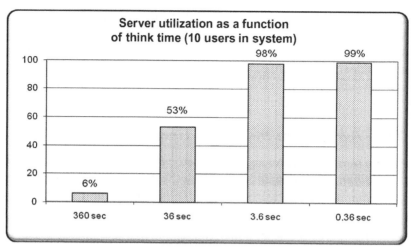

Chart 3.3.   Server utilization as a function of think time (10 users).

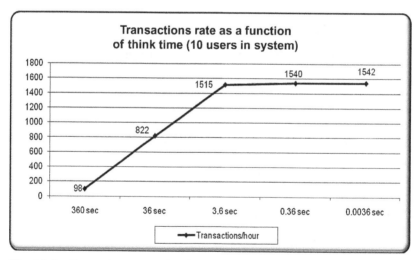

Chart 3.4.   Transaction rate as a function of think time (10 users).

or the other makes load test results and predictions of a model inaccurate and misleading.

Think time can be a parameter of choice if we want to generate a stressful workload in order to identify an application's breaking points; in such cases, a gradual lowering of think time in the load generator will increase demand for system capacity, and at some point will create a bottleneck on one of its resources. We saw in Chart 3.3 when think time was 3.6 sec, the node "Server" was maxed out reaching 98% utilization. Performance engineers have to pay close attention to think time settings in load generation tools; in some cases their default values are low, and, if they are not changed, the application undergoing the test is exposed to a stressful workload.

Take Away from the Think Time Model

- *Transaction rates and user think times impact application performance and affect utilization of system resources and transaction response times. A decrease in think time as well as an increase in transaction rate creates a more stressful workload.*
- *Realistic transaction rates and user think times have to be specified in order to provide meaningful sizing estimates and appropriate tuning of production systems.*

Workload Deviations

Tuning projects are often executed using software load generators; in such cases, first and foremost we have to pay attention to workload accuracy because it is in direct correlation with the success or failure of a tuning project. The saying "garbage in, garbage out" reflects the essential impact of workload specifications on the performance analyst's recommendations on tuning settings and hardware sizing. With the help of a model, we evaluate how a skewed workload definition might lead to the wrong decisions.

"Garbage in, Garbage out" Models

We analyze a model of an application supporting financial reporting, budget planning, and financial consolidations (Fig. 3.8).

The model includes the nodes representing one "Web" server, two "Planning" servers, two "Financial" servers, two databases ("OLAP" and "Relational"), as well as one "Consolidation" and one "Print" server. Each server has eight CPUs; an exception is the "OLAP" server, which has 20 CPUs. Table 3.2 lists all transactions as well as the nodes they visit while being processed. Symbol X in a cell located at the intersection of a transaction name and a node means that the transaction is processed in that node. Because there are two "Planning" nodes, a

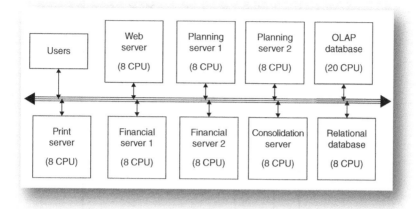

Figure 3.8. Model of a planning, reporting, and consolidation application.

transaction will be directed only in one of them by a load-balancing algorithm; the same is true for the "Financial" servers.

We analyze the model for four workloads: the first one is used as a baseline, and the other three will represent its distortions. We use the name "realistic" for the baseline workload, assuming it was observed in a real production system.

Realistic Workload

A list of transactions and their rates, as well as a distribution of 1,000 users among transactions, are presented in Table 3.3. The table specifies the realistic workload, and we will see shortly that our application is optimized for it. In the next steps we will skew the realistic workload in a few ways to get a sense of how a deviation of workload might lead to the wrong conclusions on system performance.

The modeling results in Chart 3.5 show that under a realistic workload an application represented by its model in Fig. 3.8 is satisfactorily scalable—it is capable of supporting 1,000 concurrent users with only a slight increase in transaction times, compared to the measurements for a single user.

The system is also well balanced under realistic workload, per Chart 3.6. "Planning server 1" and "Planning server 2" are utilized equally (52% each); the same is true for "Financial server 1" and "Financial server 2" (45% each). "Print," "Consolidation," and "Web"

Table 3.2
Transaction Itineraries

				Node				
	"Users"	"Web"	"Planning 1" or "Planning 2"	"Financial 1" or "Financial 2"	"Consolidation"	"Print"	"OLAP Database"	"Relational Database"
Simple report	X	X	X			X	X	X
Medium report	X	X	X			X	X	X
Complex report	X	X	X			X	X	X
Planning business rule	X	X	X				X	
Medium consolidation	X	X	X	X				X
Complex consolidation	X	X	X		X			X
Data load	X	X	X	X				X
Consolidation report	X	X		X		X		X

Table 3.3

Workload for "Garbage In, Garbage Out" Model: "Realistic Workload"

Transaction Name	Realistic Workload	
	Transaction Rate	Number of Users (1,000 Total)
Simple report	15	310
Medium report	10	90
Complex report	5	80
Planning business rules	10	150
Medium consolidation	15	140
Complex consolidation	10	60
Data load	10	70
Consolidation report	15	100

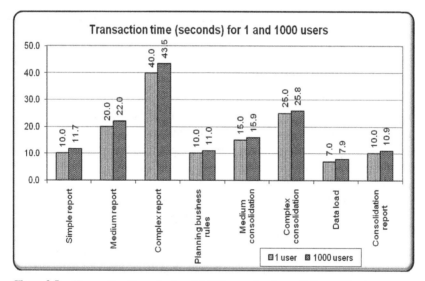

Chart 3.5. Transaction times for 1 and 1,000 users for the realistic workload.

servers have plenty of CPU capacity. The "Relational" and "OLAP" database servers are utilized at higher rates but do not create any bottlenecks in the system.

Now let's change the realistic workload to find out how deviations from its specifications affect system performance. We will skew the realistic workload in three ways: (1) redistributing users among

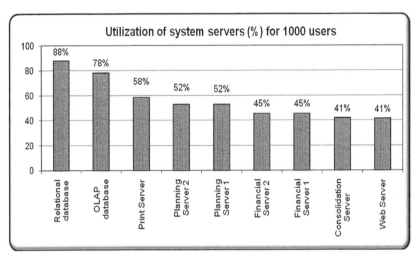

Chart 3.6. Utilization of system servers for 1,000 users.

transactions, (2) increasing the number of users, and (3) changing transaction rates.

Users' Redistribution

New user distribution among transactions is reflected in the last column of Table 3.4. We redistributed users running the "Small," "Medium," and "Complex" reports. Chart 3.7 indicates that workload redistribution leads to longer response times; for example, the transaction "Planning business rules" was increased by 63%, and the transaction "Medium report" is longer by 27%.

A reason for longer transactions is overutilization of the "OLAP" server, which is running at 97% of its CPU capacity (Chart 3.8).

Workload redistribution created a bottleneck on the "OLAP database" server, which is not present in the case of the realistic workload. If we would test the application under the redistributed workload produced by software load generator, we would recommend increasing "OLAP database" server capacity. In fact, we would advise an unnecessary expense because for a realistic workload, "OLAP database" server is sufficient.

Changing Number of Users

The next experiment with workload deviation is increasing the number of users as seen in Table 3.5. In that user-intense workload, the numbers

Table 3.4

Workload for "Garbage In, Garbage Out" Model: "Users' Redistribution"

Realistic Workload

Transaction Name	Transaction Rate	Number of Users (1,000 Total)	Number of Users After Redistribution (1,000 Total)
Simple report	15	310	160
Medium report	10	90	140
Complex report	5	80	180
Planning business rules	10	150	150
Medium consolidation	15	140	140
Complex consolidation	10	60	60
Data load	10	70	70
Consolidation report	15	100	100

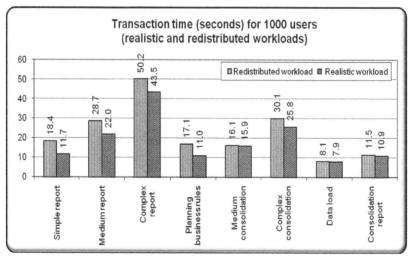

Chart 3.7.   Transaction times for realistic and redistributed workloads.

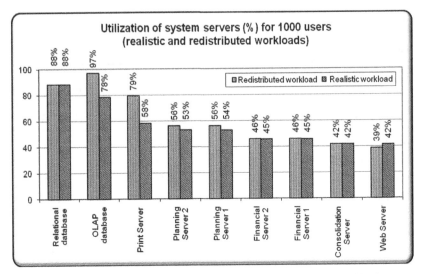

Chart 3.8. Utilization of system servers for realistic and redistributed workloads.

Table 3.5
Workload for "Garbage In, Garbage Out" Model: "Changing the Number of Users"

Transaction Name	Transaction Rate	Number of Users (1,000 Total)	Number of Users After Adding Users (1,100 Total)
Simple report	15	310	310
Medium report	10	90	90
Complex report	5	80	80
Planning business rules	10	150	150
Medium consolidation	15	140	200
Complex consolidation	10	60	100
Data load	10	70	70
Consolidation report	15	100	100

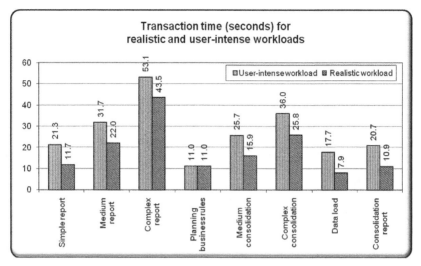

Chart 3.9.   Transaction times for realistic and user-intense workloads.

of users for transactions "Medium consolidation" has changed from 140 to 200 and for "Complex consolidation" from 60 to 100, bringing the total number of users from 1,000 to 1,100.

Professional intuition predicts longer transaction times and the model confirms that (Chart 3.9). By increasing the number of users for "Medium" and "Complex" consolidation transactions, we maxed out the "Relational database" server (Chart 3.10). The user-intense workload created a bottleneck on "Relational database" but not on "OLAP database" as in the case of redistributed workload. We have received one more confirmation that an accurate workload characterization is critical for troubleshooting application performance. By applying the wrong workload, a performance analyst might find himself in a position to recommend a cure for self-inflicted wounds but not for the real issues.

One more example of skewed workload leading to wrong prescriptions follows.

Transaction Rate Variation

Transaction rate is another workload parameter that has to be treated with caution as it has a great impact on system performance. We increased it six times for the transaction "Complex consolidation" as indicated in Table 3.6 and referred to it as the "rate-intense" workload.

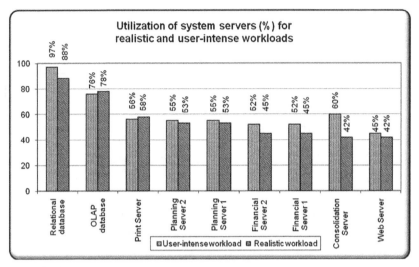

Chart 3.10. Utilization of system servers for realistic and user-intense workloads.

Table 3.6
Workload for "Garbage In, Garbage Out" Model: Transaction Rate Variation

Realistic Workload			Average Number of Transactions Per User Per Hour for Rate-Intense Load
Transaction Name	Transaction Rate	Number of Users (1000 Total)	
Simple report	15	310	15
Medium report	10	90	10
Complex report	5	80	5
Planning business rules	10	150	10
Medium consolidation	15	140	15
Complex consolidation	**10**	60	**60**
Data load	10	70	10
Consolidation report	15	100	15

After solving a model for the rate-intense workload we can compare transaction times and server utilizations with the model under the realistic workload (Charts 3.11 and 3.12).

The rate-intense workload increased "Complex consolidation" time from 25.8 sec to 79.8 sec. Under the rate-intense load there are two

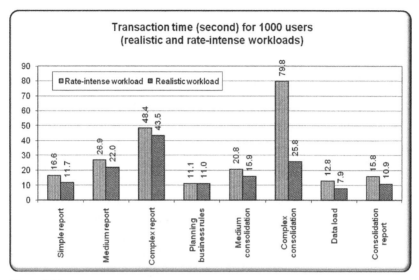

Chart 3.11. Transaction times for realistic and rate-intense workloads.

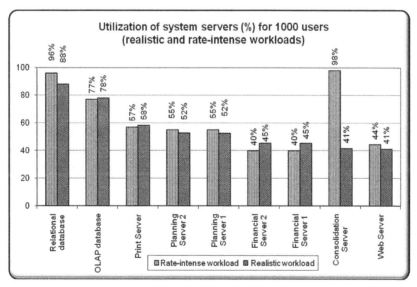

Chart 3.12. Utilization of system servers for realistic and rate-intense workloads.

bottlenecks, one on the "Relational database" server and one on the "Consolidation server" (Chart 3.12).

Take Away from "Garbage in, Garbage out" Models

- *Wrong representation of a workload leads to troubleshooting of bottlenecks created by a skewed workload and does not discover and address real performance issues.*
- *Treat a workload with utmost respect and go for its most representative specifications no matter how difficult that can be. A skewed workload ruins the entire performance project.*
- *When specifying a workload you might use realistic or any kind of purposely skewed workload depending on the project goals. You can use a stressful load to find an application's breaking points, or you might limit the workload to a few transactions to troubleshoot a particular issue. But what you cannot do is to tune and size the system under a skewed workload. If you do that, you cure self-inflicted wounds but not the real issues.*

Number of Application Users

When looking for the number of application users while characterizing a workload we have to distinguish three metrics:

- **Total number of users**. Usually this is equal to the number of users having access to the application (they have user names, passwords, and are provisioned accordingly). In some cases that number is defined by the number of licenses purchased from the application vendor.
- **Number of active users**. This is the percentage of the total number of users and represents the ones logged into the application and working with it; typically in a range of 20% to 30%.
- **Number of concurrent users**. The most intriguing of the three metrics, we analyze it below.

The question, "How many concurrent users are working with an application?" draws conflicting answers from different people. To shed

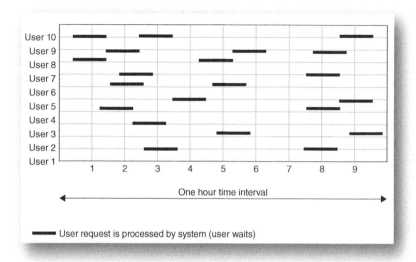

Chart 3.13.   User concurrency.

light on the issue, let's clarify what user concurrency means. As we have seen, a user interaction with an application has two components: think time (a user is not requesting any services from the system) and wait time (the system is processing the user's request). *The number of concurrent users can be defined as the number of users waiting for replies from the system to their requests.* Only concurrent users consume system resources; the users who are in think time mode do not. A system might have a fairly large number of active users, but if they interact with the system at a very slow rate, then the load on the system is low.

User concurrency is illustrated in Chart 3.13. The chart represents the activity of ten users during 1 hour. Black lines indicate the time when users' requests are processed by the system. Users demanded a different number of transactions during 1 hour; for example, user 1 submitted two requests, and user 10 submitted three requests.

Based on Chart 3.13, we can find out the number of concurrent users at different times (Chart 3.14.).

Chart 3.14 shows that the number of concurrent users is actually a random variable (in our example it changes from 0 to 4 despite having 10 active users logged into the system). The number of concurrent users

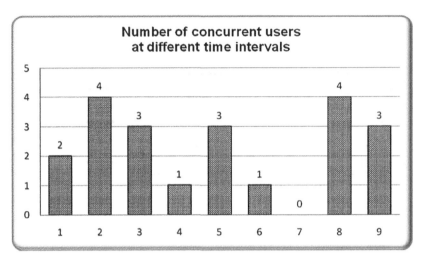

Chart 3.14. Number of concurrent users at different times.

depends on the number of active users, their think times, as well as the speed of the transaction processing by the system.

The number of concurrent users is equal to the number of users waiting for their requests to come back from the system after being processed. It depends on the total number of active users logged into the system, their think times, and the speed of transaction processing by the system.

User Concurrency Model

Queuing models are capable of calculating user concurrency. We will show it by using the model in Fig. 3.5 with two service nodes and solving it for 100 and 200 users with think times of 500 sec, 360 sec, and 180 sec (Chart 3.15).

The model reveals that user concurrency grows with the number of active users as well as when think times are getting smaller. For example, for 200 active users there are only 8 concurrent users when each user submits ~7 requests per hour (3,600 sec/500 sec think time = ~7 requests/hour). But if think time goes down from 500 sec to 180 sec (which means each user submits 20 requests per hour), then the application has 123 concurrent users.

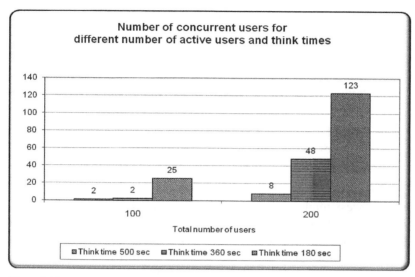

Chart 3.15. Number of concurrent users for different total numbers of active users and think times.

Take Away from User Concurrency Model

- *The users waiting for replies to their requests from the system are designated as concurrent. Only concurrent users consume system resources because the transactions they initiated are either in waiting queues or in processing units.*

- *The number of concurrent users is a function of the workload and application processing speed but not a parameter that is defined* a priori. *The number of concurrent users can be evaluated using queuing models.*

- *User concurrency increases with the growth of the number of active users as well as with the growth of the rate of transaction requests. Also, the slower the system hardware, the higher user concurrency.*

3.3. BUSINESS PROCESS ANALYSIS

In order to specify an enterprise application workload we have to analyze the business process. Instead of defining its meaning, here are a few self-explanatory examples:

- **Budgeting** (creating, analying, and approving budgets for all of the corporation's groups and departments)
- **Tracking travel expenses** (collecting travel expenses data, tracking their approvals, and crediting reimbursements)
- **Paying vendors' invoices** (verifying, entering, and paying invoices from vendors)
- **Payroll** (calculating net pays and withholdings as well as distribution of salaries by checks and electronic payments)

When we size a planned system we can start by studying the business process implemented in the organization and then adjust the collected data, taking into account the functionality of the upcoming application. If the system is already deployed and in production mode, then transaction statistics can be obtained via different data collection means: real user and transaction monitoring, parsing application log files, page tagging, etc. In some (still rare!) cases, an application can be instrumented and have a built-in functionality that accumulates transactional statistics.

Business processes can be better understood if they are presented—guess what—by their models [3.6, 3.7]. To gather transactional information, the business process model has to describe the process's steps (activities), their order, and the frequency of each step. There are different ways to model a business process, from a simple representation as a diagram up to complex and expensive modeling software. Time and cost constraints of performance tuning and sizing projects in many cases prohibit expensive and lengthy business process analysis. The performance analyst has to stick with a simple but effective approach to collect useful information; the best approach is to conduct interviews of people who know the business process the best. Usually they are business analysts whose job is implementing the process on a regular base. For instance, financial consolidations are carried out by the finance department while procurement is an activity of the purchasing department. By interviewing business experts or asking them to fill out questionnaires we might obtain realistic transaction statistics. For example, financial analysts have very good estimates of the types and numbers of financial reports they review during a work day.

For the purpose of workload specification we can formalize the business process as a diagram; such a simple representation visualizes

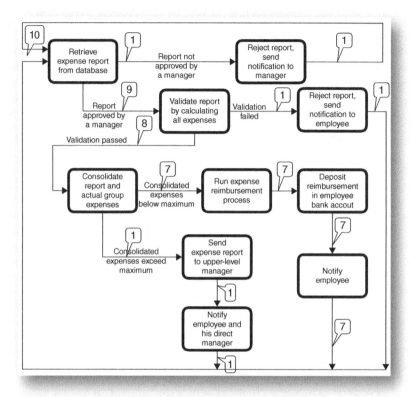

Figure 3.9. "Tracking travel expenses" business process.

sequences of activities and facilitates gathering of transaction statistics. Let's take a look at a diagram representing the business process "Tracking travel expenses" (Fig. 3.9).

The company employees submit expense reports that have to be analyzed before they are paid in order to ensure that they are in line with company reimbursement policy. A business analyst starts the process from the step "Retrieve expense report from database," which is a decision-making activity. If a manager did not approve the report, then the analyst rejects it and sends a notification. If the report is approved, the analyst verifies it by recalculating all expenses. In case verification has failed, the analyst sends a notification to the employee. If validation has passed, the analyst adds the reported expenses to the group's current expenses to make sure the actual total is within the group's allocated budget. When the budget is exceeded, expense reports get sent to a higher level manager for consideration, and a notification is sent to the employee and his direct manager. In case the actual budget is below the allocated maximum, the analyst starts the expense reimbursement procedure and initiates payment to the employee with appropriate notification. The process is repeated as many times as the number of expense reports the analyst has to process during the workday.

The diagram in Fig. 3.9 implicitly specifies the list of transactions:

- Retrieve expense report from the database
- Reject report, send notification to manager
- Validate report
- Reject report, send notification to employee
- Consolidate report and actual group expenses
- Execute expense reimbursement process
- Deposit reimbursement into employee account
- Send report to upper-level manager
- Notify employee
- Notify employee and his direct manager

After all transactions are identified we can calculate the average number of executions of each transaction by one analyst for 1 hour. We have to start from the average number of expense reports an analyst has to process during an 8-hour workday. Let's suppose his plan is 80 reports per workday; this means 10 reports per 1 hour. Not every report will be paid because some will not have a manager's approval, some won't be validated, and some are so costly that allowed expenses will be exceeded.

In Fig. 3.9, the callouts on the lines coming from the decision-making steps specify the number of expense reports that will be processed on the next step. A callout on the lines coming into the block "Retrieve expense report from database" indicates that an analyst will retrieve 10 reports from the database during 1 hour of the workday. The callouts on the lines coming out of the block "Retrieve expense report from database" note that one out of 10 reports will be rejected because they are not approved by a manager. Nine out of 10 reports will go through the validation step. Validation is also a decision-making

Table 3.7
Workload Characterization Based on Business Process Analysis

Transaction Name	Average Number of Transactions Per User Per Hour	Number of Users
Retrieve expense report from database	10	20
Reject report, send notification to manager	1	
Validate report	9	
Reject report, send notification to employee	1	
Consolidate report and actual group expenses	8	
Execute expense reimbursement process	7	
Deposit reimbursement into employee account	7	
Send report to upper-level manager	1	
Notify employee	7	
Notify employee and his direct manager	1	

process: one out of nine reports won't be validated, and eight out of nine reports will go on to the consolidation step. After consolidation, seven out of eight reports will be finally paid, and one out of eight reports will be sent to upper management for approval.

The callout numbers on incoming lines specify the average number of executions of each step per 1 hour by one analyst, which directly translates into the number of transaction executions.

To complete the workload characterization, we have to request from the business the number of users running the process "Tracking travel expenses." For example, if the answer is 20 users, than we can consolidate the workload data into Table 3.7.

We have characterized a workload for one business process; if an application supports a few business processes the same approach still applies. Let's consider an application serving two processes: financial reporting and purchase order fulfillment. Report retrieval starts from setting up report parameters: year, location, and product (Fig. 3.10). If the parameters values are, respectively, 2008, New York, and Soda, it means the analyst wants to get information on soda sales volume in New York in year 2008 across all company stores. After that, the analyst requests report retrieval. Usually two out of 10 reports are printed out as the hard copy documents, which is indicated by callouts.

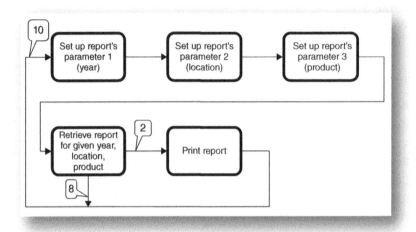

Figure 3.10. "Financial reporting" business process.

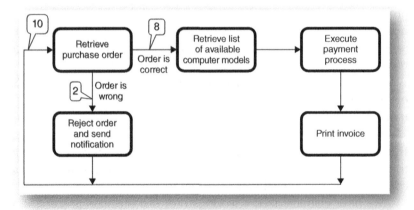

Figure 3.11. "Purchase order fulfillment" business process.

Purchase order fulfillment starts from retrieving an order from the database and reviewing it (Fig. 3.11). On average, only eight out of 10 orders are submitted without any errors, and two out of 10 orders are rejected as they do not have the correct information. Correct orders are processed by executing payments and printing final invoices.

Table 3.8
Workload Characterization for Two Concurrent
Business Processes

Transaction Name	Average Number of Transactions Per User Per Hour	Number Of Users
Process "Financial reporting"		
Set up report's parameter 1 (year)	10	25
Set up report's parameter 2 (location)	10	
Set up report's parameter 1 (product)	10	
Retrieve report	10	
Print report	2	
Process "Purchase order fulfillment"		
Retrieve purchase order	10	40
Reject order and send notification	2	
Retrieve list of available computer models	8	
Execute payment process	8	
Print invoice	8	

Per information from the diagrams in Figs. 3.10 and 3.11, and after getting the numbers of users running each process from the business, we can fill out Table 3.8 with workload characterization data.

It should be noted that in a case of two concurrent processes, the total number of business analysts is $25 + 40 = 65$.

Interaction with business experts can be formalized and structured using questionnaires. The simplest one might have just one question: "Describe what you are doing to accomplish a particular task (for example, 'Purchase order fulfillment')." The question starts a conversation, which, if properly conducted by a performance analyst, will provide the workload specification. Tables 3.7 and 3.8 are actually examples of very compact questionnaires.

Business process analysis helps characterize workload. A business process can be described best by business specialists who implement it regularly; they have to be interviewed by the performance analyst to specify workload.

3.4. MINING TRANSACTIONAL DATA FROM PRODUCTION APPLICATIONS

Working with a production system provides an opportunity to obtain realistic statistics on workload and transaction profiles by digging out bits and bytes of information from various log files maintained by an application as well as by using transaction monitoring software.

We examine both avenues, but first we describe how to measure a transaction profile by using free and readily available monitoring tools and utilities that are built into operating systems.

Profiling Transactions Using Operating System Monitors and Utilities

All operating systems are instrumented, which means they maintain software counters that collect metrics for performance analysis of different objects (processors, processes, disks, memory, etc.). Monitors and utilities built into operating systems read counters and make the data available for examination. Data can be presented as charts on a graphical interface similar to Windows Performance Monitor or reported in text format as the majority of UNIX utilities do. Data are also available on the programming level, and all third-party commercial monitors extract it and convert it into informative and easy-to-examine graphs, charts, and reports. Monitors and utilities built into an operating system give insight into system-related metrics, but they are incapable of doing the same for application transactions. Additional steps are needed to obtain transactional information; we explain them for Windows Performance Monitor, but the same technology is applicable to all UNIX flavors.

1. Ensure that you are the only user of the application and that no background process is or will be running while you profile the transaction.

2. If possible, set up the load generator to initiate a transaction multiple times by a single user. If a load generator is not available, be ready to do it yourself. In our experiment only a single transaction is processed by the application; that means the transaction does not wait in any application queues.

3. Identify all hardware servers a transaction visits while being processed.

4. For each hardware server, identify a **process** that is being executed while handling transaction. In that context, a **process** is
an instance of a computer program that is currently active on
a hardware server dealing with the transaction [3.8]. In the
Windows environment, running processes are displayed by
the task manager (Fig. 3.12). In UNIX environments, a number
of commands report a list of processes (Fig. 3.13 shows an output

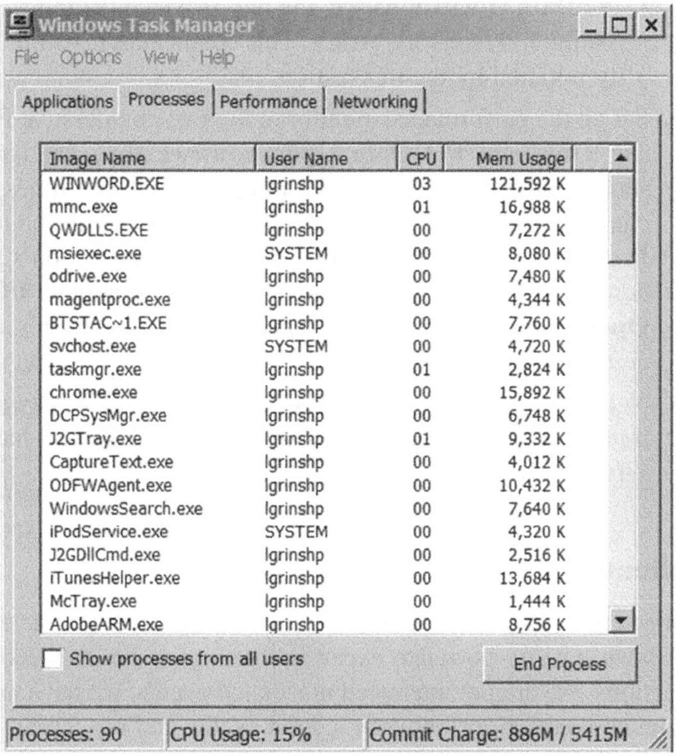

Figure 3.12. Running processes reported by Windows Task Manager.

```
PID    USERNAME   SIZE    RSS STATE  PRI NICE     TIME CPU PROCESS
11672 hypadmin    88M    41M cpu40     0   12  7:15:49 6.2% ESSBASE/13
  575 root        19M    12M sleep    59    0 56:44:17 1.2% fmd/23
11832 hypadmin  2008K  1696K cpu0     59    0  0:00:00 0.0% prstat/1
  150 root      4704K  3720K sleep    59    0  0:00:00 0.0% picld/5
  275 root      2864K  1248K sleep    59    0  0:00:00 0.0% cron/1
  266 root      1984K   768K sleep    59    0  0:00:00 0.0% sckmd/1
```

Figure 3.13. Running processes reported by UNIX command **prstat−a**.

of the **prstat –a** command). For each **process**, the operating system maintains counters that measure its utilization of CPUs as well as the I/O system while serving the transaction. The time interval when the utilization counter is nonzero represents a transaction service demand. To measure it we have to monitor two counters:

- **% Processor Time**: the percentage of elapsed time that the transaction uses the CPUs.
- **I/O Data Operations/sec**: the rate at which the transaction is issuing I/O reads and writes. This counter counts all I/O activity initiated by the transaction.

5. Set up the performance monitor to log two counters: **% Processor Time** and **I/O Data Operations/sec** for each hardware server and execute a single transaction multiple times. Build charts from log file data. The time interval when the counter **% Processor Time** is nonzero represents the transaction's service demand for a CPU. The time interval when the counter **I/O Data Operations/sec** is nonzero represents a transaction's service demand for the I/O system.

6. Network service demand is equal the difference between the transaction response time and service demands in all hardware servers.

Application Log Files

Making sense out of log file information requires time and determination, as we have to correlate excavated data to trace and reconstruct transactions. We are not interested in isolated events; we have to establish logical connections between logged events and synchronize them in time so they can be associated with particular transactions. Invoking our car-transaction metaphor, we have to find the car's itinerary by looking for car traces in log files. In some cases, that means sifting through huge volumes of data saved in different log files on different servers of distributed systems.

The most popular and extensively studied source of data is the Web server log file. An applied science called "Web analytics" has emerged from Web log files analysis [3.9, 3.10]. The Web log, among other information, keeps statistics on the number and types of requests sub-

```
111.111.111.111 - [2/May/08 - 00:23:48] "GET /reportAAA.HTML"
123.123.123.123 - [2/May/08 - 00:23:48] "GET /reportBBB.HTML"
222.222.333.444 - [2/May/08 - 00:25:48] "GET /formAAA.HTML"
333.333.333.333 - [2/May/08 - 00:25:55] "GET /formBBB.HTML"
444.444.444.444 - [2/May/08 - 00:26:01] "GET /consolidationAAA.HTML"
555.555.555.555 - [2/May/08 - 00:26:03] "GET /login.HTML"
```

Figure 3.14.   Web server log file.

mitted by users. Let's take a look at an example of a truncated simplified log file that has information we need for workload characterization (Fig. 3.14). The fragment shown identifies five users who are accessing the application from different computers (IP addresses 111.111.111.111, 222.222.222.222, and so on). For each user, the log file has a time stamp with date and time of access, as well as a URL that defines the business transaction requested by the user.

Using that information, it is possible to find out the number of each transaction's executions during particular time intervals. This oversimplified Web log file example demonstrates the availability of the information needed for workload specification. To obtain such information from fully populated production log files, we have to use commercial strength log file analyzers because the size of the log files preclude nonautomated parsing. Moreover, a system might have a few Web servers, and in that case, information has to be collected from a number of Web log files and correlated.

Figure 3.15 demonstrates the log file maintained by an enterprise application that implements financial consolidations. The reported information has transaction names, their start and stop times, the name of the hardware server that carried out the transactions, as well as consolidation details.

Transaction Monitors

Transaction monitors are the most informative tools that supply transactional statistics for workload characterization and transaction profiling. Oracle's Real User Experience Insight [3.11] implements user session monitoring and business transaction tracking. The monitoring capability is built using network protocol analysis technology, which

User	Activity	Time Start	Time End	Server	Description
user0001@LDAP	Logoff	3/28/2011 12.12	3/28/2011 12.12	ConsolServer25	
user0001@LDAP	Consolidation	3/28/2011 12.02	3/28/2011 12.12	ConsolServer25	Completed Scenario Actual, Start Period Oct, End Period Dec, Entity ABCD, Parent DFGRE, year 2010
user0001@LDAP	Logon	3/28/2011 12.02	3/28/2011 12.02	ConsolServer25	
user0001@LDAP	Logoff	3/28/2011 12.02	3/28/2011 12:02	ConsolServer25	
user0001@LDAP	Consolidation	3/28/2011 11:57	3/28/2011 12:02	ConsolServer25	Completed Scenario Actual, Start Period Apr, End Period Dec, Entity DMNI, Parent BFGTS, year 2010
user0001@LDAP	Logon	3/28/2011 11:57	3/28/2011 11:57	ConsolServer25	
user0001@LDAP	Logoff	3/28/2011 11:57	3/28/2011 11:57	ConsolServer26	
user0001@LDAP	Consolidation	3/28/2011 11:47	3/28/2011 11:57	ConsolServer26	Completed Scenario Actual, Start Period Jun, End Period Aug, Entity ONVFR, Parent LOKNN, year 2010
user0001@LDAP	Logon	3/28/2011 11:47	3/28/2011 11:47	ConsolServer26	
user0001@LDAP	Logoff	3/28/2011 11:47	3/28/2011 11:47	ConsolServer25	
user0001@LDAP	Consolidation	3/28/2011 11:46	3/28/2011 11:47	ConsolServer25	Completed Scenario Actual, Start Period Feb, End Period Jul, Entity ABC, Parent MNGR, year 2010
user0001@LDAP	Logon	3/28/2011 11:46	3/28/2011 11:46	ConsolServer25	
user0001@LDAP	Logon	3/28/2011 11:45	3/28/2011 11:45	ConsolServer25	

Figure 3.15.   Financial consolidation server log file.

does not require modification, changes, or instrumentation of the application. Correlsense's SharePath [3.12] recognizes transaction type (e.g., "login," "send_money," "buy_stock," etc.), which tiers are utilized, and measures time spent on each tier (e.g., Web, application, database, etc.). Transactional data collected by SharePath is compatible with Metron's capacity planning applications (http://www.metron-athene.com) and can be feed directly into the model. CoreFirst by OpTier [3.13] reports which business transactions are being processed by each server and tier. CoreFirst treats transactions as composed of multiple work units that are executed on application tiers such as Web, application, and database servers. The product employs proprietary technology to associate in real time all work units with the logical business transactions to which they belong.

All of above and similar transaction monitoring offerings position themselves in a product category "business transaction management." In addition to collecting data on the performance of hardware components, they also report workload characterization, transaction profiles, and correlate transactional and hardware performance metrics. Proponents of the category consider it an evolution and enhancement of the older and more mature "hardware performance management" product group. As consumers of both transactional and hardware performance metrics, we only benefit from such development.

Insightful information on workload characterization in various environments can be found in a variety of publications [3.14, 3.15, 3.16, 3.17, 3.18].

TAKE AWAY FROM THE CHAPTER

- *Application workload is the flow of transactions initiated by users forcing the application to do some amount of work in order to generate replies; workload characterization includes three components:*
  - *List of business transactions*
  - *For each transaction, the number of users requesting it*
  - *For each transaction, the number of its executions at particular time intervals (usually during 1 hour) per requests from one user; that number is called the transaction rate.*
- *Wrong characterization of a workload leads to troubleshooting of bottlenecks created by a skewed workload and does not discover nor address real performance issues; a skewed workload ruins the entire performance project. You might use a purposely skewed workload (e.g., a stressful one to find an application's breaking points), but never tune and size a system under a skewed workload.*
- *The users waiting for replies from the application are designated as concurrent. Only concurrent users consume system resources because the transactions they initiated are either in waiting queues or in processing units.*
- *A transaction profile represents the set of time intervals (service demands) a transaction has spent in all processing units it has visited while served by the application.*
- *Workload can be characterized by analyzing a business process. Its parameters, as well as transaction profiles, can be found by using monitors and utilities that are built into operation systems, and by examining various log files. Commercial transaction monitors are the most informative tools that supply transactional statistics.*

## CHAPTER 4

Servers, CPUs, and Other Building Blocks of Application Scalability

In this chapter: application scalability; modeling CPU bottlenecks and studying how to eliminate them by using additional CPUs and servers as well as faster CPUs; modeling I/O bottlenecks and analyzing the ways to fix them by using additional and faster disks; considerations on the impact on application performance by popular hardware technologies (multi-core CPUs, hyper-threaded CPUs, storage area networks).

4.1. APPLICATION SCALABILITY

Enterprise applications are designed as scalable objects: They can accommodate an increase in the number of users and in the volume and complexity of data without transaction time degradation by using additional CPUs, servers, and other hardware components. Scalability is not only an application's attribute; scalable objects and processes surround us. In the summer, airlines add more flights to popular vacation

Solving Enterprise Applications Performance Puzzles: Queuing Models to the Rescue, First Edition. Leonid Grinshpan.
© 2012 Institute of Electrical and Electronics Engineers. Published 2012 by John Wiley & Sons, Inc.

destinations. During peak hours, additional tollbooths are open on highways. Phone companies announce from time to time that more lines are added to accommodate growth in the number of service subscribers; they also increase the speed of the phone lines.

> Application scalability is its ability to maintain an acceptable (as defined by the users) transaction time under an increasing workload by utilizing additional or faster hardware components (servers, CPUs, etc).

There are two ways to scale the application. We can **scale an application vertically (scale up)** by *replacing* the current hardware with higher-grade hardware (in terms of speed, throughput, latency, etc.). Examples of vertical scaling are servers with faster CPUs, faster disks, and lower network latency. Vertical scaling requires more expensive equipment. Alternatively, we can **scale an application horizontally (scaling out)** by *adding* more hardware of the same or even lower grade. Examples of horizontal scaling are adding servers, adding disks, or adding network lines. Horizontal scaling might be less expensive as it is often based on commodity equipment.

4.2. BOTTLENECK IDENTIFICATION

The complexity of enterprise applications requires nontrivial efforts to ensure proper scaling. In order to find out which hardware resource has to be scaled, an application has to be exposed to a load from a number of users or forced to process a large volume of data; monitoring the application under such circumstances identifies the hardware components that cause bottlenecks. The collected data may indicate that performance degradation is due to a shortage of CPU capacity, inadequate I/O speed, scarce network throughput, etc.

In this chapter we will learn how to identify bottlenecks caused by limited hardware capacity; we will use the model in Fig. 4.1 to evaluate different approaches to fixing hardware bottlenecks. The model represents the simplest system setup that hosts all the application's layers

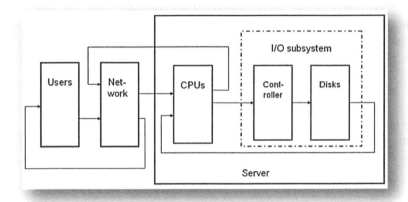

Figure 4.1. Model with CPU and I/O subsystem.

on one server; we intentionally are using a simple model as it helps to focus on scaling effects without diverting attention to the model's intricacies.

Unlike previous models, this one lets us take into consideration the server's "internal" specifications by modeling its CPUs as well as the components of the I/O subsystem (controller and disks) by separate nodes. Such a greater level of detail allows us to examine conditions that create bottlenecks on CPUs and I/O subsystems.

A transaction initiated by a user arrives over the network at the server's CPU and initiates an I/O operation that transmits data to or from disks. Two major parts of the I/O system are the I/O controller and disks. The I/O controller manages data transfer by orchestrating and synchronizing I/O operations over a bus connecting all the components of the I/O subsystem. The disks provide storage for data.

By including new nodes in the model we can evaluate the impact of the I/O controller and disk specifications on application performance. From a performance perspective, the I/O controller is characterized by the **Bus Transfer Rate**, usually measured in megabytes/second, as well as by the time needed to manage I/O operations. That time is called **Controller Overhead**.

The disk's main parameter is **Disk Access Time**, which has two components: the time a transaction has spent in the controller (controller service demand) and the time the transaction was served in the disk (disk service demand) during one I/O operation.

CPU Bottleneck

A CPU bottleneck can be identified by monitoring a server's CPU utilization as well as the CPU queue. The main indicator is **% Processor Time**, which measures the percentage of total server utilization. If this counter exceeds 85–90%, then noticeable CPU queues are building up. Readings of that counter let us find out how many CPUs are in use. First we have to calculate the contribution of each CPU to total server utilization per the formula:

$$100\% \, / \, N,$$

where N is the number of a server's CPUs.

For two-CPU servers, each CPU contributes 50%; for four CPUs, the contribution is 25%; for eight CPUs, it is 12.5%. Second, we calculate the number of busy CPUs for a given **%Processor Time**:

$$(\%Processor\ Time * N) \, / \, 100\%.$$

For example, if **%Processor Time** = 37.5% for an eight-CPU server, then three CPUs are working at their maximum capacity.

Server queues are monitored by a counter called the **Processor Queue Length**. Processor queues exceeding two or three requests have a great impact on transaction times and indicate that a server has reached the capacity limit of all its CPUs. A CPU bottleneck can be fixed by increasing CPU speed, adding CPUs, or adding a server.

CPU Bottleneck Models

CPU bottleneck models help us to learn how to discover a CPU bottleneck, as well as how to fix it by adding CPUs or servers, or by using faster CPUs. We will use the model in Fig. 4.1 as a starting point and analyze the variations of that model with different numbers of CPUs, servers, and CPU speeds.

CPU Bottleneck Identification. We start from the model in Fig. 4.1 and assume that it has two CPUs, one disk controller, and four disks. That configuration represents the baseline model that we will later change to analyze different ways to scale hardware.

The workload and transaction profile for the baseline model are defined in Table 4.1.

Transactions are processed by CPUs, network, controller, and disks. The workload for the model comprises interactive transactions;

Table 4.1

Workload and Transaction Profile for CPU Bottleneck Model

Workload			Transaction Profile			
					Disk Access Time	
Transaction Name	Number of Users	Transaction Rate	Time in Node "Network"	Time in Node "CPUs"	Time in Node "Controller"	Time in Node "Disks"
Interactive transactions	Model solved for 100, 200, and 300 users	15	0.05 sec	2.0 sec	0.03 sec	0.1 sec

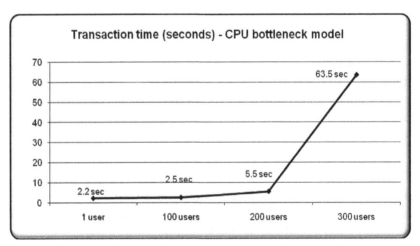

Chart 4.1. Transaction times—baseline model.

for a single user in a system, a transaction time is 0.05 + 2.0 + 0.03 + 0.1 = 2.18 sec.

After solving the baseline model for 1, 100, 200, and 300 users, we have built Chart 4.1 with transaction times for different numbers of users.

The response time gets longer starting from 200 users; we got the classic "hockey stick" effect as the transaction time jumped more than

10 times. Transaction time increase is due to a saturation of CPUs—for 300 users total utilization reached 98.8% (Chart 4.2).

Chart 4.3 shows that a CPU queue length was more than four requests for 200 users and reached over 60 requests for 300 users.

Modeling results confirm that a CPU bottleneck exposes itself by high CPU utilization and CPU queues.

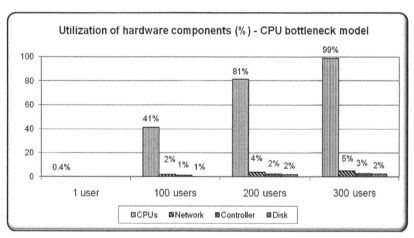

Chart 4.2.   Utilization of system hardware (%)—baseline model.

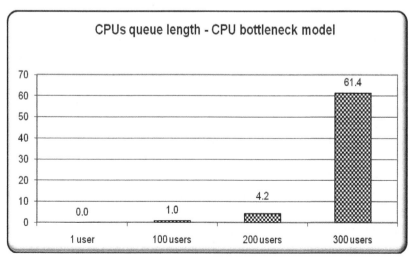

Chart 4.3.   CPU queue length—baseline model.

Additional CPUs. Let's fix a CPU bottleneck by increasing the number of CPUs. We added two, six, and 14 CPUs to the existing two CPUs and analyzed the model. Transaction times for systems with two, four, eight, and 16 CPUs are presented in Chart 4.4.

Adding CPUs permits the system to support more users. The hockey stick patterns in Chart 4.4 indicate a limit in the number of users that a system with a particular number of CPUs is capable of supporting without transaction time degradation. Time degradation takes place when a server reaches between 80% and 85% of its CPU capacity. Vertical lines correlate hockey sticks with server utilization. For example, for four CPUs, response time degradation happens when the number of users exceeds 400; at that moment, server utilization is above 80%.

Additional Servers. Let's analyze how additional servers can expand a system's capacity. The model in Fig. 4.2 features two servers; we will also analyze a system with three servers. All the servers in this model have the same specifications as in the baseline configuration: each one has two CPUs, one disk controller, and four disks.

Delivered by the model, transaction times for a system with one, two, and three servers (Chart 4.5) indicate that scaling the system horizontally by adding servers resolves the CPU bottleneck. As more servers are added, the more users a system can support with a given service level.

Our models indicate that scaling out CPU capacity can be achieved either by adding CPUs or by adding servers. The question of which way is more preferable cannot be answered by the models; the correct answer can be found taking into account not only the formal modeling predictions, but also economic, organizational, and other real-life constraints. It is very important to keep in mind that any horizontal scaling includes additional management overhead: The more hardware components a system has, the more time is needed to organize and schedule processing of user transactions. The impact of management overhead on system performance is discussed in Chapter 5.

Faster CPUs. Vertical scaling of a server's CPU capacity is achieved by using faster CPUs. In our theoretical study we have the freedom and flexibility (not always available in reality) to speed up our baseline model's two CPUs. Speeding up CPUs makes transaction time shorter because processing in a CPU takes less time. Let's presume that our *Faster CPU model* has CPUs that are twice as fast as the baseline

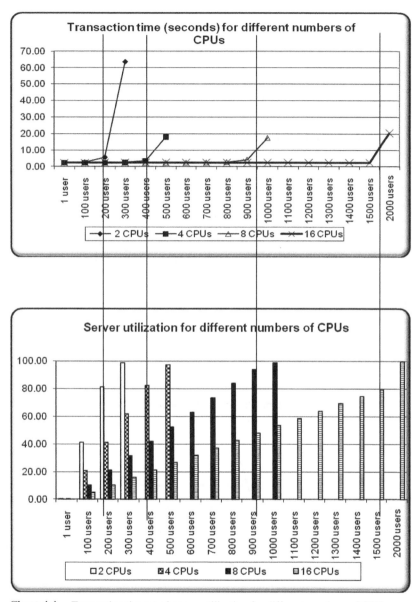

Chart 4.4. Transaction times and server utilization for different numbers of CPUs.

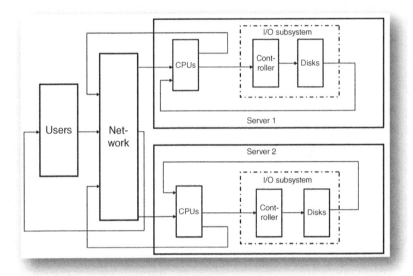

Figure 4.2. Model with two servers.

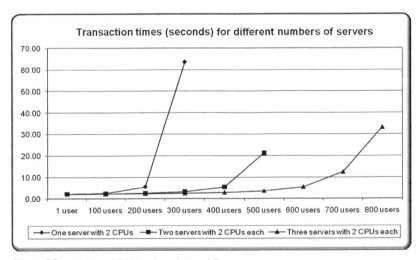

Chart 4.5. Fixing a CPU bottleneck by adding servers.

model (the time in node CPU is 1.0 sec vs. 2.0 sec in the baseline model). The model predicts that the faster CPU improves transaction time as well as accommodates more users (Chart 4.6).

As expected, time improvement disappears even for the faster CPU as soon as the server hits a CPU bottleneck. For 400 users, transaction time will deteriorate and exhibit the familiar hockey stick effect.

A speed comparison of different CPUs is based on standardized benchmarking procedures (www.spec.org) and tends to take into account multiple factors that influence CPU processing capacity. Among those factors are CPU architecture, clock speed, command set, internal caches, and other technology-specific features. In addition to those factors, the specifics of applications greatly impact CPU capacity, which makes a speed comparison even more complicated. For example, some CPUs are designed for particular business tasks, such as online transaction processing when a large user community generates transactions that require short processing time. Using servers with such CPUs for applications that implement analytical calculations will compromise system performance. For that reason, CPU benchmark data should be used with application specifics in mind and be considered only as a starting point when evaluating relative CPU capacity.

With the onset of new technologies such as multi-core CPUs and hyper-threading CPUs [4.1], we have to be even more careful when

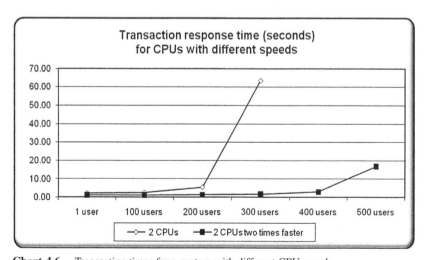

Chart 4.6.   Transaction times for a system with different CPU speeds.

evaluating CPU capacity. Multi-core CPUs consist of a number of CPUs located on the same silicon circuit, and in many cases they are not fully independent because they share some components. For example, a silicon circuit hosting eight cores might have only one floating-point unit; in such a case, an analytically intense application will still have limited available capacity. Hyper-threaded CPUs expose themselves to operating system configuration utilities and monitors as an object with one CPU per thread. That means, for instance, that for an eight-CPU server, Windows Task Manager will report eight CPUs when hyper-threading is turned OFF and 16 CPUs when hyper-threading is ON. In actuality, by enabling hyper-threading, the capacity of the CPU might increase only from 10% to 30%, but not two times, as someone might conclude based on Task Manager information; it even can degrade for some applications. When building models we have to take into account only the CPU capacity an application can use; that means a performance engineer has to educate himself on an application's functionality and its specifics in order to have clear understanding of application demand for hardware resources. Garmatyuk [4.2] analyzes the impact of additional cores and hyper-threads on CPU capacity for different programs: 3D visualization, 3D rendering, scientific and engineering analysis, raster graphics, data compression, compiling, audio and video encoding, Java Virtual Machine benchmark SPECjvm2008, 3D games.

Garmatyuk's conclusions are applicable to a particular tested configuration, but nevertheless they provide impressive examples of how application specifics can benefit (or suffer) from CPU technologies. Because enterprise applications are often running on Java Virtual Machine, results of benchmark SPECjvm2008 on a single CPU platform are of particular interest: (1) performance gain when turning ON hyper-threading is 21–27%; (2) performance gain when adding a second core is 77–92%.

Take Away from the CPU Bottleneck Model

- *To identify a CPU bottleneck we have to monitor CPU utilizations and server queues; metrics to monitor are **%Processor Time** and **Processor Queue Length**. We can be certain that there is a CPU bottleneck if CPU utilization consistently exceeds 85% and server queues consistently go above three or four requests.*

- *A CPU bottleneck can be fixed by adding more CPUs to a server; a system with additional CPUs is capable of supporting more users without transaction time degradation. The number of CPUs is limited by the state of technology.*

- *A CPU bottleneck can be also fixed by adding servers; potentially the number of servers is unlimited.*

- *Horizontal scaling brings additional management overhead. The more hardware components a system has, the more time is needed to organize and schedule processing of user transactions. For that reason, the growth of CPU capacity is not linear, as additional CPUs or servers are included in the system. As an example, we cannot expect that doubling the number of CPUs or servers will double the number of users a system can serve with an acceptable service level.*

- *Vertical scaling of CPU capacity is based on using faster CPUs. Unlike scaling out by adding servers, technology dictates the limits of this approach. Speeding up CPUs makes transaction time shorter because processing in a CPU takes less time.*

- *The benchmark data on CPU speed should be considered only as a reference point when evaluating relative CPU capacity; an application's specifics have a major impact on relative CPU speed and must be taken into account.*

I/O Bottleneck

One of the indicators of an I/O bottleneck is a high reading of the counter **%Disk Time**, which can be interpreted as the percentage of time a disk is busy servicing read/write operations. When **%Disk Time** exceeds 80–85%, disk queues will result; the queues can be monitored by the counter **Disk Queues Length**. Disk queues slow down transactions that request I/O operations if they exceed two to three waiting transactions.

Another cause of I/O operations slowness can be found by examining the counters **Disk Read Bytes per Second** and **Disk Write Bytes per Second**. Both counters report the rates of data transmission between system memory and disk; if any of those values are low, then read or write operations are slow. The qualification of the values as "low" can be made on a relative, but not absolute, base. That means the values have to be compared with the readings for different transactions, or with the ones for the systems hosted on different hardware platforms. A comparison is also possible if software or hardware changes affecting I/O operations were implemented; in such a case, "before and after" measurements are available to support the right conclusions.

The above counters can be analyzed for physical as well as for logical disks; however, the means to fix a bottleneck differ. In a case where a logical disk is reaching its maximum utilization, but a physical disk has unused capacity, we can create additional logical disks on the same physical one. If a physical disk is overutilized, however, then adding more physical disks is the only way to fix an issue.

I/O Bottleneck Models

By using I/O bottleneck models we will analyze how to identify an I/O bottleneck, as well as how to fix it by adding disks or using faster disks. We continue to use the model from Fig. 4.1 and solve the variations of that model with different numbers of disks as well as different disk speeds.

I/O Bottleneck Identification. The workload and transaction profile for the model in Fig. 4.1 are defined in Table 4.2; the workload is intentionally specified as more I/O demanding.

Table 4.2 describes a workload similar to a CPU bottleneck model, but to make the I/O impact more pronounced we increased service times in node "Disks" from 0.1 sec to 2 sec and decreased service time in node "CPUs" from 2 sec to 0.1 sec. Such a transaction profile is common in I/O-intense applications.

The model represents a system with two CPUs, one disk controller, and four disks, and we consider it as a baseline I/O bottleneck model that we are going to modify in different ways to analyze various scenarios.

As the baseline model shows, transaction time started to deteriorate for 400 users, and became very long for 500 users (Chart 4.7).

Disk utilization (Chart 4.8) suggests that transaction time degradation is due to a significant demand for disk services for 500 users because the disks are running at almost 100% of their capacity.

Chart 4.9 shows that disk queue length reaches more than five requests for 400 users and that causes transaction time to grow exponentially.

Table 4.2
Workload and Transaction Profile for the "I/O Bottleneck Model"

Workload			Transaction Profile			
					Disk Access Time	
Transaction Name	Number of Users	Transaction Rate	Time in Node "Network"	Time in Node "CPU"	Time in Node "Controller"	Time in Node "Disks"
Interactive transactions	Model solved for 100, 200, and 300 users	15	0.05 sec	0.1 sec	0.03 sec	2 sec

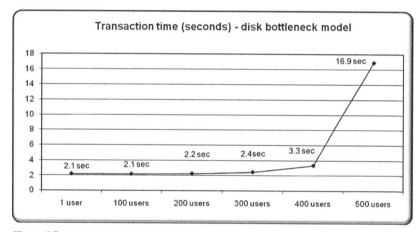

Chart 4.7.   Transaction times—disk bottleneck model.

The model demonstrates that an I/O bottleneck is present when the disk is utilized above 85% of its capacity and has a waiting queue of more than two or three requests.

Additional Disks. Scaling an I/O system by adding one disk eliminates the bottleneck, as can be seen from Charts 4.10 and 4.11; utilization of the disks dropped to under 85%. Adding more disks will scale the I/O system, making it capable of supporting more than 500 users without response time degradation. The I/O controller can maintain a limited number of disks; adding more disks might require additional I/O controllers.

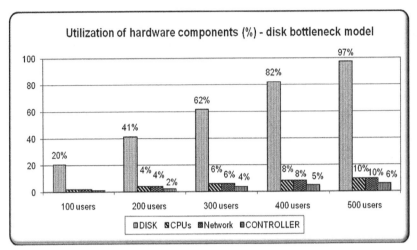

Chart 4.8. Utilization of system hardware (%)—disk bottleneck.

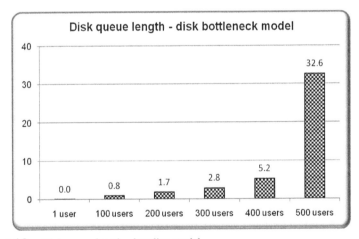

Chart 4.9. Disk queue length—baseline model.

Faster Disks. The time a single transaction is served in node "Disks" greatly depends on the size of data transferred to and from the disk during the transaction, as well as on the speed of the read/write disk operations. If the transaction reads N bytes from the disk, then the time it will spend in node "Disks" can be calculated by the formula:

Time in node "Disks" = N/Disk Read Bytes per Second.

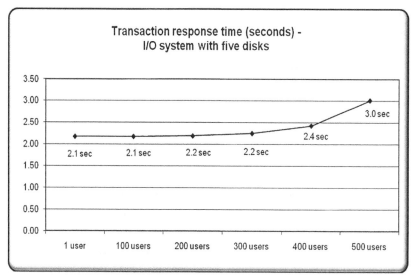

Chart 4.10. Transaction response time; system with five disks.

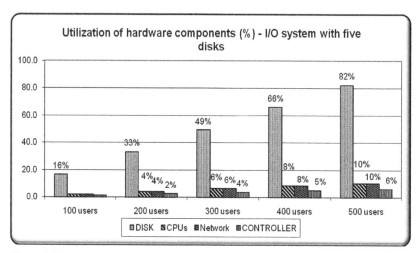

Chart 4.11. System utilization; I/O with five disks.

The formula allows us to analyze how disk speed impacts system performance. Let's assume that a 2-sec time in node "Disks" (which we are using in the baseline I/O models; see Table 4.2) was calculated for a transaction reading 2 MB of data from the disk with a speed of 1 MB/sec. In the *Faster disk* model, we will analyze how an increase in disk speed to 1.05, 1.1, 1.2, and 1.5 MB/sec translates into better system performance. Per our formula, time in node "Disks" is getting shorter as disk speed increases (we read the same 2 MB of data):

Time in Node "Disks" (sec)	Disk Speed (MB/sec)
2	1
1.9	1.05
1.81	1.1
1.66	1.2
1.33	1.5

We solve the model for different disk speeds; the impact of disk speed on transaction time can be seen in Chart 4.12.

Disk speed at 1.2 MB/sec eliminates a disk's bottleneck, delivering transaction times of fewer than 4 sec for up to 500 users. A faster disk with a data transfer speed at 1.5 MB/sec enables the system to serve not 500 but 600 users efficiently.

Disk speed is represented by transfer time or transfer rate in the documentation of some vendors and in several benchmarks. If we know the transfer rates for a number of disk varieties, we can evaluate

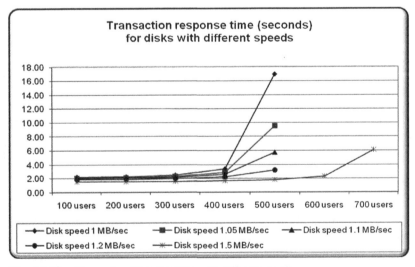

Chart 4.12.   Transaction times for disks with different speeds.

hardware architectures with different disks, local as well as connected over networks. One of these (very popular in enterprise application deployments) varieties is the storage area network (SAN). Our I/O models seamlessly expand to that kind of storage because SANs are designed in a way that they appear to the hardware server as local disks. The growing acceptance of the SAN as a component of the enterprise application infrastructure makes our I/O models the indisposable instruments for assessment of a SAN's impact on system performance. Data on SAN speed can be found in benchmarks published by the Storage Performance Council (http://www.storageperformance.org). Benchmark SPC-2 evaluates the performance of storage subsystems during the execution of business-critical applications with intense I/O operations initiated by three workloads:

- Large file processing: Applications that require simple sequential processing of large files such as scientific computing and large-scale financial operations.
- Large database queries: Applications that involve data mining or business intelligence.
- Video on demand: Applications that streamline video from a digital film library.

For each workload, the SPC-2 benchmark provides the rate of data transfer in megabytes/second for only read, for only write, and for a combination of read/write operations. Based on those metrics, it is easy to calculate **Disk access time** for I/O models. An example of metrics reported by the SPC-2 benchmark is shown in Fig. 4.3.

Take Away from the I/O Bottleneck Model

- *To identify an I/O bottleneck we have to monitor disk utilizations and disk queues; metrics to monitor are %Disk Time and Disk Queue Length. An I/O bottleneck exists if a disk's utilization consistently exceeds 85% and the disk's queues go over two or three requests.*
- *Logical disk space limitations can be fixed by increasing its size if a hosting physical disk has additional capacity.*

SPC-2 Reported Data				
IBM TotalStorage™ SAN Volume Controller 3.1				
SPC-2 MBPS™	SPC-2 Price-Performance	ASU Capacity (GB)	Total Price	Data Protection Level
3,517.75	$563.93	20,615.843	$1,983,784.74	Mirroring

The above SPC-2 MBPS™ value represents the aggregate data rate of all three SPC-2 workloads: Large File Processing (LFP), Large Database Query (LDQ), and Video On Demand (VOD)

SPC-2 Large File Processing (LFP) Reported Data				
	Data Rate (MB/second)	Number of Streams	Data Rate per Stream	Price-Performance
LFP Composite	2,707.28			$732.76
Write Only:				
1024 KiB Transfer	1,295.21	96	13.49	
256 KiB Transfer	1,414.87	96	14.74	
Read-Write:				
1024 KiB Transfer	2,366.74	96	24.65	
256 KiB Transfer	2,502.02	96	26.06	
Read Only:				
1024 KiB Transfer	4,259.25	96	44.37	
256 KiB Transfer	4,405.58	96	45.89	

The above SPC-2 Data Rate value for LFP Composite represents the aggregate performance of all three LFP Test Phases: (Write Only, Read-Write, and Read Only).

SPC-2 Large Database Query (LDQ) Reported Data				
	Data Rate (MB/second)	Number of Streams	Data Rate per Stream	Price-Performance
LDQ Composite	4,385.76			$452.32
1024 KiB Transfer Size				
4 I/Os Outstanding	4,257.44	96	44.35	
1 I/O Outstanding	4,394.06	96	45.77	
64 KiB Transfer Size				
4 I/Os Outstanding	4,455.87	96	46.42	
1 I/O Outstanding	4,435.66	96	46.20	

The above SPC-2 Data Rate value for LDQ Composite represents the aggregate performance of the two LDQ Test Phases: (1024 KiB and 64 KiB Transfer Sizes).

SPC-2 Video On Demand (VOD) Reported Data				
	Data Rate (MB/second)	Number of Streams	Data Rate per Stream	Price-Performance
	3,460.23	4,400	0.79	$573.31

Figure 4.3. Metrics reported by the SPC-2 benchmark for the IBM TotalStorage appliance.

- *Physical disk bottlenecks can be fixed by either adding hardware (horizontal scaling) or by using faster disks (vertical scaling).*
- *I/O system speed is measured in the number of bytes it writes to and reads from a disk per 1 sec. Transactions that include read/write operations spend some time in an I/O system; this time can be calculated by dividing the volume of data a transaction transfers over the I/O system by the I/O system speed measured in the number of bytes transferred every second.*

TAKE AWAY FROM THE CHAPTER

- *An appropriately designed application can be scaled to accommodate an increase in the number of users and volume and complexity of data without compromising transaction time. Horizontal scaling is implemented by adding hardware components (servers, CPUs, disks, etc.); vertical scaling is enabled by employing faster hardware components.*

- *Analyzed CPU and I/O bottleneck models bring to light the relationship between application performance and horizontal and vertical scaling.*

- *Application design and functionality have to be taken into account to understand to what extent multi-core and hyper-treading CPU technologies affect the application's performance.*

## CHAPTER 5

Operating System Overhead

In this chapter: components of operating systems; the system time model; the impact of system overhead on transaction time and hardware utilization.

5.1. COMPONENTS OF AN OPERATING SYSTEM

Any computer system has four main components: hardware, applications, users, and operating system (Fig. 5.1).

The operating system (OS) is the highest management authority: it receives requests for services from all the components and assigns and schedules appropriate resources to satisfy all the requests. Figure 5.2 provides a generalized view of the functions an OS carries out per requests from other components. We limit discussion of OS functionality only to the topics directly related to OS overhead; for a conceptual overview of OS design, including the latest developments in OS technologies please refer to Tanenbaum [5.1] and Silberschatz [5.2].

Requests from users are generated when users operate input devices such as keyboard, mouse, and touch screens. These user-induced requests do not reach the application directly even though their final

Solving Enterprise Applications Performance Puzzles: Queuing Models to the Rescue, First Edition. Leonid Grinshpan.
© 2012 Institute of Electrical and Electronics Engineers. Published 2012 by John Wiley & Sons, Inc.

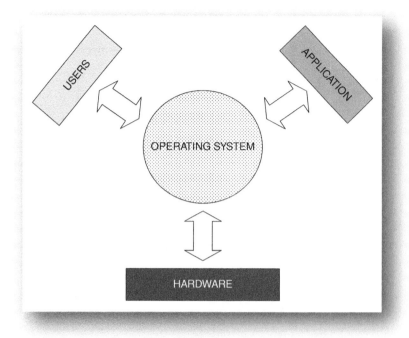

Figure 5.1.   Interaction among system components.

destination is the application. It is well known that each device has its driver; it might be less known that each driver is a part of the OS. A request from an input device goes directly to the OS, which invokes the appropriate driver to process it. A driver directs a request to an application ONLY if the application is in an active mode running on a CPU. If the application is waiting for a CPU's time slice or for an I/O operation, a driver will keep the request waiting.

The separation of users' requests from the application allows the OS to fulfill its main goal—managing the computer system by allocating its resources according to priorities set up by a system administrator. Usually the OS is in charge of maximizing computer system throughput; that means the OS strives to enable as much data processing as possible at any given time by utilizing all available hardware. The OS does not let any single user or process monopolize time or resources: The OS "turns on" a green light for any request only if and when its fulfillment is in line with OS management policies.

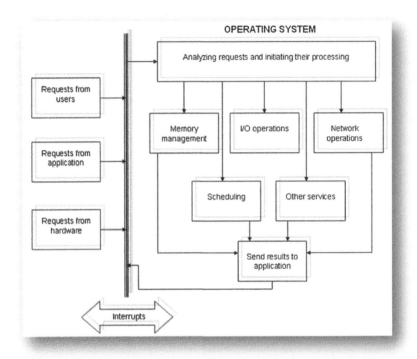

Figure 5.2. OS functions.

The same "separation" rule applies not only to users' requests but also to applications. Applications cannot initiate any I/O operations or reallocate memory; they have to ask the OS to carry out I/O or network operations, to allocate additional memory, and to perform a variety of non-hardware-related services. Hardware equipment requires OS attention when it has completed any operations per the demand from users and applications. Another group of I/O requests is generated by devices that react to the variety of events external to the computer system. The representative examples are temperature and pressure meters, motion detectors, timers, multiple sensors reporting the status of printers connected to the server, scanners, and faxes. The OS takes care of each demand and transfers control to the appropriate application according to scheduling algorithms.

The OS is positioned on a crossroad among users, applications, and hardware; it enables communication among all the components and synchronizes their cooperation. Each component notifies the OS of its needs by initiating an **interrupt**—a process of transferring control from the users, application, and hardware to the OS. The OS transfers control back to the components when the request's processing is completed. When an interrupt happens, the OS analyzes what service was requested and launches the appropriate management subsystem to satisfy the request according to a schedule. The OS manages memory allocations, I/O and network operations, and implements sophisticated scheduling algorithms in order to maximize utilization of system resources. In addition, the OS provides numerous general services making the software development process more productive; that means that if a program needs a function implemented in the OS, all a programmer has to do is to include in its code a call to the OS function. That call will initiate an interrupt, and the OS will execute requested function.

For example, when a program needs an I/O operation (let's say reading data from a disk), it calls the OS requesting the specified data from a specified logical disk. The OS accepts the request and lets the program continue its execution until the requested data are available. At the same time, the OS initiates the I/O operation, which might be executed concurrently with the program. By delegating the handling of I/O operations to the OS, a computer system is capable of executing a program on CPUs and at the same time transferring data to/from external devices as demanded by the same program. Moreover, it enables concurrent execution of a few programs on the same server and the sharing of I/O devices among them; this concept is called "multiprogramming."

It is quite obvious that the OS takes time to satisfy each and every request; because the OS is a program, it also uses hardware resources to execute requests. That means that we pay a price for OS service. The price is the time the OS uses the system's hardware to implement its functions. This time is called **system time**, and it represents a system overhead.

The operating system (OS) is the highest computer system management authority that (like any other software component) consumes system resources to implement its functions.

5.2. OPERATING SYSTEM OVERHEAD

System overhead can be quantified by measuring the following main characteristics:

- The time when requests are processed by the OS (called **system** or **privileged time**; this is different from **user time**, when requests are processed by the application).
- Rate of switches between system time and user time (**context switches per second**). A context switch occurs when any of the events that initiate an interrupt happen.
- Rate of calls from the application to the OS for services; it is usually measured in the number of **system calls** per second.
- The activity of hardware devices is reflected in two metrics: the **number of interrupts** coming from all devices every second and the percentage of elapsed time spent by the OS for servicing hardware interrupts (often called **interrupt time**).

System overhead can be observed using monitoring utilities that vary from OS to OS. The main metrics made available by Windows Performance Monitor are:

- **%Privileged (System) Time**: percentage of elapsed time when all requests are processed by the OS.
- **%Interrupt Time**: percentage of elapsed time spent for servicing interrupts generated by hardware (keyboard, mouse, system clock, network interface card, storage devices, etc.).
- **Interrupts/sec**: rate of interrupts coming from hardware devices.
- **Context Switches/sec**: the combined rate at which all CPUs on the computer are switched among threads. Multithreaded architecture is pervasive in enterprise applications because it enables an application to initiate and execute multiple tasks independently of each other [5.3]. This is not an all-inclusive list of the functions multithreaded applications support: serving requests from multiple users; running transaction processing in a CPU concurrently with I/O operations; breaking down large operations (such as financial consolidation) into a few tasks and executing

them independently. An object that is running each task in a multithreaded environment is called a thread. Threads need access to a CPU or I/O system to process a task; because many threads are competing for resources, the OS allocates limited time for a thread to use a resource. When the time expires, the OS saves all the data from memory and internal CPU registry pertaining to the thread (context) and starts another thread on the same resource, loading its context. This process is called "context switch." The fewer hardware resources (for example, CPUs) an OS handles, the more often it has to enact a context switch to accommodate all threads.

- **System Calls/sec**: these represent the combined number of calls to OS services by all running processes; an application initiates such a call when it needs a service to be performed by the OS. An example of the most frequent system call is a request to perform an I/O operation.

When analyzing system overhead for a particular OS and hardware platform, it is necessary to become familiar with the description of each counter as the interpretation of data they provide is system specific.

What causes the growth of system overhead? Here are the main contributors:

- **Number of users.** Higher numbers of users leads to more interrupts at any given time because there are additional active input devices. A very important factor is the transaction rate; a higher rate means every user generates transactions more often, which leads to extra interrupts.

- **Number of CPUs.** Managing more CPUs and allocating and scheduling application execution among a higher number of CPUs drives system overhead up. This is, by the way, one of the reasons why increasing the number of a server's CPUs N times does not increase its total CPU capacity N times.

- **Number of servers.** If an application is hosted on server farms, the OS coordinates activities across multiple servers, load balancers, and hardware appliances per application demand. Different OSs have specific components for interserver communication. Network load balancing services (NLBS) is Windows' component that manages clustering and load balancing and provides high availability, reliability, as well as scalability (http://technet.microsoft.com/en-us/library/bb742455.aspx). A similar Solaris component is called IPMP, or IP network multipathing; it arranges fault-tolerance and load distribution (http://download.oracle.com/docs/cd/E19455-01/806-6547/). The clustering environment for AIX and Linux is offered by the IBM Reliable Scalable Cluster Technology (RSCT) module (http://www.redbooks.ibm.com/abstracts/tips0090.html?Open).

- **Number of concurrently running applications.** Each application is asking the OS for services; the more applications that are hosted on the same computer the higher the number of system calls, which translates into higher overhead.

- **Application algorithms.** The intensity of an application's requests to the OS for services depends on application functionality. For instance, if an application needs a record saved on disk it can request the OS to load into memory 1,000 records by one I/O operation, or it can initiate through the OS 1,000 I/O operations, each one reading one record. In this simple example, the better option is obvious; software developers face not-so-evident choices.

- **Settings of an application's tuning parameters.** An application's tuning parameter values define the intensity of requests that have to be satisfied by the OS. In general, a tuning parameter defines a quantity of a particular resource (for example, the number of connections to a database); reassigning resources per application requests always involves OS activity.

- **Complexity of an I/O system.** Each component of an I/O system is managed by the OS; more components mean a higher rate of demands from the I/O system that have to be satisfied by the OS.

- **Network connections.** A network is permanently full of life; data travel across it even if no users are active and the OS has to serve network interrupts.

To get an idea of the values of OS overhead counters, let's take a look at Table 5.1; it has data collected for a laptop running the Windows XP 32-bit OS and a server running the Windows Server Standard 64-bit

Table 5.1
OS Overhead Counters

	Laptop 1 CPU 2 Cores, 2.66 GHz, 4 GB RAM Idle Mode	Server 4 CPU 2 Cores, 3.5 GHz, 12 GB RAM	
		Idle Mode	Under Load from 25 Users
Number of running processes	85	81	81
Number of running services	0	145	145
%Privileged time	4.2	0.5	4.5
%Interrupt time	0.06	0.02	0.9
Interrupts/sec	175	8,200	12,500
Context switches/sec	5,108	2,100	3,400
System calls/sec	20,500	190,000	230,000

OS when both computers were idle (that means they were booted up but did not serve any users), as well as when the server was under load from 25 users.

A first look at the data indicates that the OS never sleeps. Even when there is no user activity, the OS performs its management duty. The server in idle mode features a much higher rate of interrupts and system calls than the laptop because it has more complex hardware architecture as well as running 145 services while the laptop runs none. The context switches rate is two times lower on the idle server, which points to the more efficient handling by the Windows Server Standard 64-bit OS than by Windows XP 32-bit OS.

When the server is under the user's load, all counters are higher; for instance, the counter **%Privileged Time** grows nine times, from 0.5 to 4.5. The OS overhead tends to increase for systems with more complex hardware and application architecture. System architecture is getting more sophisticated with each additional CPU, server, hardware appliance, storage device, as well as with additional software functionality. The number of users is a substantial contributor to OS system time. Total system overhead also adds up in virtual environments where a few virtual machines are hosted on the same server; in such environments instead of one OS there are a few OSs running concurrently (one OS per virtual machine) as well as a hypervisor.

The more components a system has and the more complex they are, the higher the OS overhead; the complexity of components depends on their architecture, software algorithms, number of connections and threads, workload, etc. A significant contributor to OS overhead is the demand for its services that is generated by the application.

We resort to the models to evaluate OS overhead impact on application performance.

System Time Models

To take into account OS management overhead we have to break the time each transaction is served in a processing unit into two elements—the time an application processes a transaction (*time in a user mode*) and the time when the OS implements management and service functions for that transaction (*time in privileged mode*).

We build and solve a model with two nodes: "Users" and "Server" (Fig. 5.3).

We reduced the complexity of the enterprise application architecture to one server with one processing unit. We also reduced the workload to one transaction; this simple model is sufficient for analysis of management overhead.

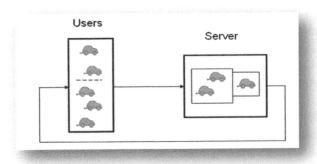

Figure 5.3. System time model.

System overhead increases the time a transaction is processed by the servers; we take that time into account in the model by increasing the time a transaction spends in the processing unit of node "Server."

Impact of System Overhead on Transaction Time

We analyze the model for three sets of input data: (1) a theoretical baseline case when overhead does not exist; (2) adding 5% to the transaction time in node "Server"; (3) adding 7% to the transaction time in node "Server." In real systems, management overhead might increase that time from a single digit percentage point to 10–40% depending on the complexity of the hardware architecture and the workload generated by the users.

We are going to analyze the overhead impact on transaction time for different numbers of users. Workload and transaction profile for the *System time model* are defined in Table 5.2.

The model shows that a system's overhead impact on transaction time increases as the number of users grows (Chart 5.1).

The contribution of system overhead to transaction time can be quite noticeable (Chart 5.2).

Overhead impact is much more evident when the server is close to saturation: for 160 users, 7% overhead contributes 6.8 sec or 50% to transaction time; for 80 users, the contribution is below 1 sec. We definitely have to pay a hefty price for system management, and the price is higher when the system is working close to its capacity limit.

Table 5.2

Workload and Transaction Profile for the Model "System Time"

Workload			Transaction Profile
Transaction Name	Number of Users	Transaction Rate	Time in Node "Server"
No system overhead (baseline)			
Transaction A	10, 20, 40, 80, 160	10	2 sec
System overhead 5%			
Transaction A	10, 20, 40, 80, 160	10	2.1 sec
System overhead 7%			
Transaction A	10, 20, 40, 80, 160	10	2.14 sec

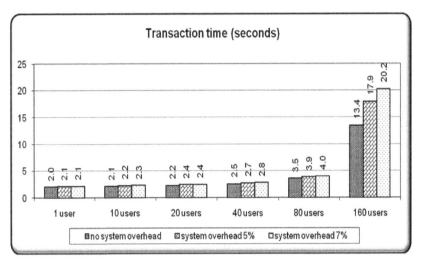

Chart 5.1. Transaction time for different system overheads.

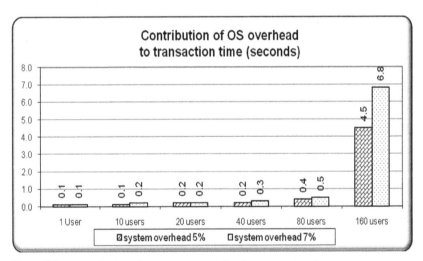

Chart 5.2. Contribution of management overhead to transaction time.

Impact of System Overhead on Hardware Utilization

Using the *System time model* and workload as defined in Table 5.2, we can assess consumption of hardware resources by the OS. The percentage of a server's utilization by the OS can be seen in Chart 5.3. The general trend illustrated by the polynomial line indicates the growth of the OS share in server utilization as the number of users increases.

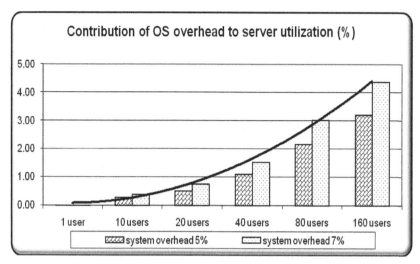

Chart 5.3. Contribution of management overhead to server utilization.

Each OS has an impressive number of tuning parameters; publications dedicated to OS tuning offer recommendations on parameter settings and methodologies of finding their optimal values [5.4, 5.5, 5.6]. OS tuning usually is performed by a system administrator with the main goal of increasing server throughput. If the server is shared among a number of applications, such tuning might not benefit our application. If the application is the only one hosted on the server, then OS tuning can be helpful, but the extent of performance improvement might be minimal because, as our analysis shows, a significant contributor to OS overhead is the demand for its service generated by the application. For that reason, before engaging in OS tuning in order to improve application performance we have to make sure that the application itself operates in an OS-sensitive mode; this means the application implements efficient algorithms and has rational settings of its own tuning parameters (more on that in the next chapter).

TAKE AWAY FROM THE CHAPTER

- *We pay a price for the services provided by the OS; the price is an increase in the transaction times and higher utilization of a system's hardware components.*

- *When analyzing application performance, always monitor OS activity by observing the counters reporting* **Privileged Time**, **Interrupt Time**, **Interrupt rate**, **Context Switch rate**, *and* **System Calls**, *as well as other OS-specific indicators; they might reveal an opportunity to improve system performance by minimizing management overhead.*

- *The impact of overhead on transaction times evidently is more negative when the system is working close to its capacity limit.*

- *To minimize OS overhead we have to use the simplest architectural and system management solutions as long as they deliver the required service level. The "simplest" means as few servers and appliances as possible, as well as the most "economical" settings of an application's tuning parameter.*

- *A significant contributor to OS overhead is demand for its service generated by an application. Before engaging in OS tuning in order to improve application performance, make sure the application itself operates in OS-sensitive mode, which means it implements efficient algorithms and has rational settings of its own tuning parameters.*

## CHAPTER 6

Software Bottlenecks

In this chapter: what is a software bottleneck; memory bottleneck models; thread optimization models; bottlenecks due to transaction affinity; limited number of database connections and user sessions.

6.1. WHAT IS A SOFTWARE BOTTLENECK?

In this chapter we analyze bottlenecks that expose themselves in a different (and sometimes more challenging) way than maxing out a server's CPUs or I/O system. We break them down into two groups:

- **Group 1.** Bottlenecks caused by the settings of application tuning parameters that limit its ability to use available hardware capacity to satisfy the workload. Bottlenecks of that group can be fixed by changing the values of the tuning parameters.
- **Group 2.** Bottlenecks caused by software algorithms and data structure deficiencies. Such bottlenecks require redesign either of an application's code or data organization.

We refer to both groups as *software bottlenecks* as they are not caused by limited hardware resources, and such a designation lets us

Solving Enterprise Applications Performance Puzzles: Queuing Models to the Rescue, First Edition. Leonid Grinshpan.
© 2012 Institute of Electrical and Electronics Engineers. Published 2012 by John Wiley & Sons, Inc.

distinguish them from *hardware bottlenecks* discussed in previous chapters.

Software bottlenecks are caused either by the settings of an application's tuning parameters or by application design deficiencies.

Let us consider a useful parallel between Group 1 of software bottlenecks and the traffic jam each of us often experiences while crossing toll plazas (Fig. 6.1).

The cars arrive at the toll plaza from different directions and they are jammed in approaching lanes because the plaza has too few lanes. As soon as a car gets through the jam it immediately finds an idle tollbooth. Increasing the number of toll booths cannot improve the plaza's throughput; what will do the trick is adding approaching lanes (Fig. 6.2.). More lanes dissolve traffic congestion and keep tollbooths busy.

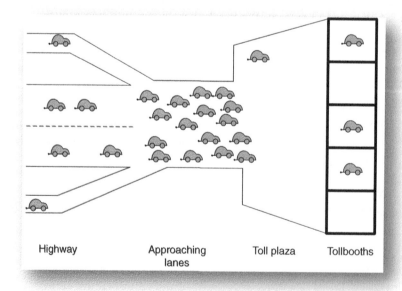

Figure 6.1.   Traffic jam at toll plaza.

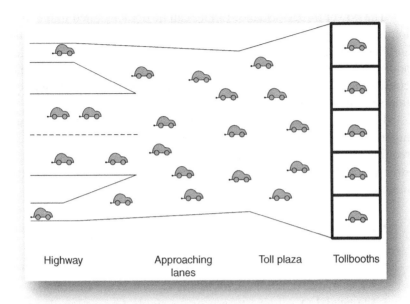

Figure 6.2. Traffic jam is fixed by increasing the number of approaching lanes.

What constitutes an application's "approaching lanes"? They are the application's tuning parameters with settings that prevent the application from using available hardware resources to their full extent. The most common parameters are:

- Memory size an application can use
- Number of threads to parallelize data processing
- Number of connections to database
- Number of sessions with interactive users

Some applications have more specific parameters as dictated by their nature:

- The number of CPUs or servers a particular process can be executed on
- The number of queued requests
- The time a request is waiting to be processed

The power of performance tuning can be demonstrated in the most impressive way by fixing Group 1 bottlenecks simply by changing the software parameter values. There is no need to spend extra money on additional hardware, no cumbersome system reconfiguration, no time-consuming redesign of algorithms or data structure, just new application settings and the problem is gone.

It is not so for the Group 2 bottlenecks; their detection is the worst nightmare for the application development team because fixing them requires a redesign of the application itself or a change in the data structure and volume. Here is how Group 2 bottlenecks might expose themselves:

- Long CPU time to process a single transaction due to inefficient software algorithm
- High I/O activity to process a single transaction due to the transfer of a large volume of data
- Elevated I/O activity to process a single transaction due to a disproportionate number of I/O operations
- Excessive intensity of application requests to the OS while waiting for an event

Group 2 bottlenecks usually happen for a very limited number of users. As an example, let's assume that the processing of one transaction takes 5 min on a server, and it loads one server's CPU at 100%; if a server has eight CPUs, then processing of eight concurrent requests will max it out. The probability of eight concurrent requests is quite high if the number of system users is in the range of hundreds. Increasing the number of CPUs is not the answer. For example, bringing the number of CPUs to 16 by adding eight more CPUs will not sufficiently decrease the probability of 16 concurrent requests. The real solution would be to minimize processing time from 5 min to 5 sec and that can be done only by redesigning the application or data structure.

Resolving a Group 2 bottleneck necessitates changes in the application and data. Usually only the application development team is capable of finding and implementing new solutions. Sometimes performance improvement can be achieved by modifying the business process. For example, it might be acceptable to the business to separate batch and interactive processes in time by allowing execution of database updates only at night and letting interactive users access the system only during the workday.

In dealing with Group 1 bottlenecks, the first solution that comes to mind is to fix the issues once and for all by setting up all tunable application parameters to the values that allow for maximum consumption of each resource and by the same token eliminate any chance of bad performance no matter what workload is generated by the users. That straightforward approach does not work and this is why: By increasing the values of Group 1 parameters we allow an application to consume more resources and (as we have seen in Chapter 5) to generate a higher management overhead. This makes the application work slower and inefficiently. The performance analyst always has to evaluate the impact of tunable parameter settings on application performance and look for the values that deliver acceptable response times. The models in this chapter enable analysis of interrelations among tuning parameters and application performance and help to devise a methodology of identifying and fixing software bottlenecks.

6.2. MEMORY BOTTLENECK

Memory constitutes a very important system resource; if a memory size requested by an application exceeds its availability, transaction times will degrade. The interaction of an application with memory is logically simple: When an application needs additional memory it sends a request to the OS to allocate memory. A request gets satisfied if memory is available; otherwise it is rejected and the application waits. A wait for available memory contributes to transaction time. When the application does not need the memory space any more, it notifies the OS. The memory gets released and the pool of free memory is increased. An application usually requests additional memory when the number of active users grows or when it processes a large volume of data and the allocated memory is too small.

An obvious memory bottleneck happens when available physical memory reaches its limit. This bottleneck is easy identifiable by monitoring free physical memory (on the Windows platform it is usually displayed on the Windows Task Manager front panel).

We will model and analyze two more challenging memory bottlenecks: (1) the application has a preset upper memory limit and the limit is reached (an example of preset memory limit is Java virtual machine maximum heap size); (2) the application permanently initiates I/O operations to read or write the pages from/to disks. This effect is called *paging*.

If the application has reached an upper memory limit, its request for additional memory can be satisfied only after reorganization of already allocated memory; that restructuring process contributes to transaction time. In the realm of Java virtual machines there is a process called *garbage collection*, which periodically deletes from memory unused objects, thereby making more memory available. Memory paging adds time to a transaction because of transfer of data to/from a disk, and it generates an additional load on the I/O system.

In order to find out memory size allocated at any given time to an application, we have to monitor the appropriate counters for the application's processes. The names of the counters vary depending on the OS; in a Windows environment the readings are provided by the counters **Private Bytes** and **Working Set**.

For applications that serve multiple users, the size of memory grows when more users actively interact with the system. A typical curve of memory utilization by an application, depending on the number of users, is pictured in Chart 6.1:

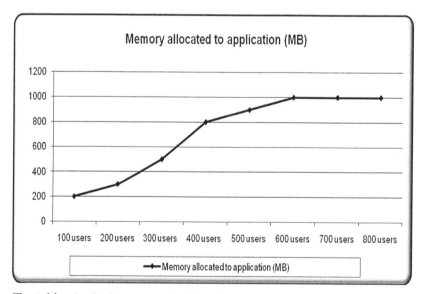

Chart 6.1. Application memory size depending on the number of users.

In our example, an application's memory size grows as more users are active; it flattens out when memory reaches its preset limit at 1,000 MB. Transaction times for a population exceeding 600 users will be longer because more time will be spent to reallocate memory.

A preset application memory limit is usually lower than a server's physical memory; in such a case, a preset limit can be increased and the bottleneck fixed. This is what happens when the upper limit of the Java virtual machine heap size is increased. When increasing the memory limit, we can hit another barrier even if there is plenty of physical memory—the limit set by the OS. For example, for 32-bit operating systems the limit is usually 2 GB per process (it might be increased to 3 GB if special settings are enabled).

The intensity and volume of data transfer between memory and disk indicates an activity associated with virtual memory. To quantify that activity we have to measure the intensity of **page faults** representing the events that happen when data cannot be found in memory, and the OS memory manager initiates an I/O operation with the disks. Page faults are very harmful for performance. The time to retrieve data from memory mostly depends on *memory access time*, which on average is from 5 to 70 nanoseconds. The time to retrieve data from a disk depends on *disk access time*, which is in a range from 2 to 7 milliseconds (2,000,000–7,000,000 nanoseconds). That means that page faults slow down access to data about 30,000–100,000 times.

Memory Bottleneck Models

Preset Upper Memory Limit

To analyze memory bottlenecks we reuse the model described in Chapter 4 in Fig. 4.1; for convenience we reproduce it again here as Fig. 6.3.

The model represents a system that hosts all application's layers on one server. The model factors in CPUs and components of I/O subsystem (controller and disks) by separate nodes. A transaction initiated by a user is processed in the network, at the server's CPU and I/O subsystem. The I/O controller implements data transfer management; the disks provide storage for data.

The workload and transaction profile for the model are defined in Table 6.1. We assume that the application's upper memory limit is preset to 1 MB, and we solve the model for different amounts of

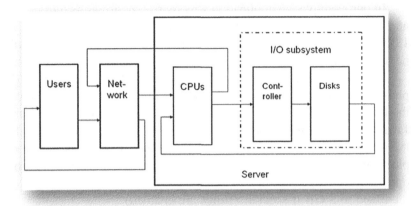

Figure 6.3. Model with CPU and I/O subsystem.

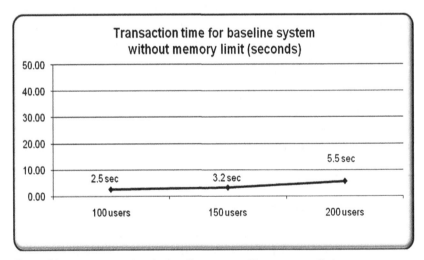

Chart 6.2. Transaction time for baseline system without memory limit.

memory required by one transaction: 200 KB, 500 KB, 700 KB, and 900 KB.

We start the analysis from a hypothetical baseline system that does not have an upper memory limit; that system has a response time under 6 sec for the number of users from 100 to 200 (Chart 6.2).

Now let's impose a memory limit. By solving the model, we can see (Chart 6.3) that for 150 users, response time degradation starts when transaction requests require 700 KB of memory; for 200 users, time degradation becomes evident when a transaction needs 500 KB.

Table 6.1
Workload and Transaction Profile for Model With Upper Memory Limit

Workload			Transaction Profile				
					Disk Access Time		
Transaction Name	Number of Users	Transaction Rate	Time in Node "Network"	Time in Node "CPUs"	Time in Node "Controller"	Time in Node "Disks"	RAM Size Allocated to One Transaction (Kb)
Interactive transaction	100, 150, 200, 300	15	0.05 sec	2 sec	0.03 sec	0.1 sec	200, 500, 700, 900

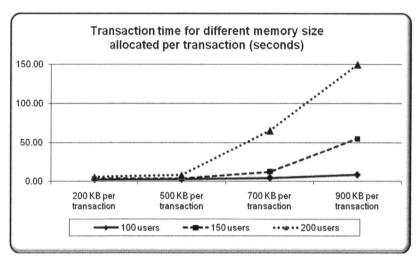

Chart 6.3.   Transaction time for a system with a 1 MB memory limit.

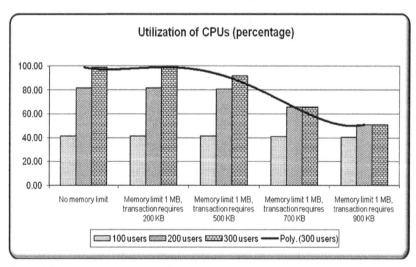

Chart 6.4.   CPU utilization for different numbers of users with a 1 MB memory limit.

The impact of a memory limit on CPU utilization might be surprising at first (Chart 6.4). For 200 users (and even more obvious for 300 users), CPU utilization drops from 81–98% to 50% as the size of memory per transaction increases from 200 KB up to 900 KB (see the trend line in Chart 6.4). A decline in CPU utilization indicates that the application cannot quickly process transactions because it has to allocate memory to each transaction from a pool that has an upper limit and is in use by other requests. That means there is a wait time for available memory; when a transaction is waiting for memory it does not need CPUs, and the CPUs have idle capacity. Actually, memory bottlenecks offload all hardware components (I/O, network, etc.) for the same reason, not just CPUs.

For 100 users, CPU utilization stays flat across Chart 6.4 (at a level a little above 40%); that is an indication that for the workload generated by 100 users, the system can efficiently handle memory allocation/release without hitting the memory upper limit.

Taking into account a decline in server utilization when reaching the memory limit, we can devise practical guidelines to identify memory shortage. For illustration we will consider only a case when each transaction requests 900 KB of memory.

In order to identify a memory bottleneck we have to apply to the application dynamic load with an increasing number of users. As we know, a load can be generated by load testing tools or a real system can be monitored under different loads. We will observe insignificant growth of transaction time until the load reaches some critical number of users and then transaction time will start growing sharply (in Chart 6.5 the "hockey stick" effect occurs for 100 user).

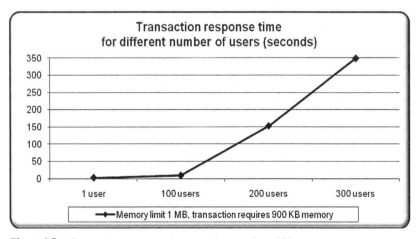

Chart 6.5. Transaction response time growth starts from 100 users.

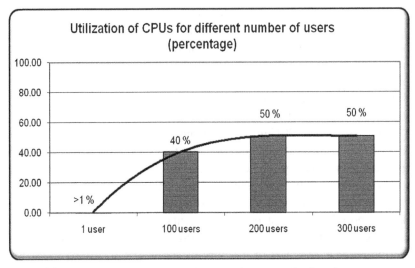

Chart 6.6. CPU utilization flattens out because of a memory bottleneck.

If CPU utilization stays flat at a level well below 100% as the number of users grows (Chart 6.6), and if transaction time starts increasing exponentially (Chart 6.5), we have a memory bottleneck.

Memory size counters provide an indication of a possible memory shortage when their readings reach the maximum values set up for the application. However, additional analysis as described above has to be carried out to make a final verdict on memory bottleneck. The reason is that the memory size counter might show an upper limit even if the application no longer needs that memory; it means that memory is not requested by other applications, and the OS does not have to reallocate it until memory is claimed. What we just described is the so-called lazy memory management algorithm employed by the OS in order to minimize system overhead.

Paging Effect

In this section we analyze paging impact on transaction time when the number of users and the paging rate change. Paging rate is measured in the number of pages transferred between disk and memory for one transaction. This is how the paging rate can be calculated: If we assume that a transaction requires 10 MB of data to be swapped into memory and one I/O operation transfers 10 KB of data, then 1,000 I/O

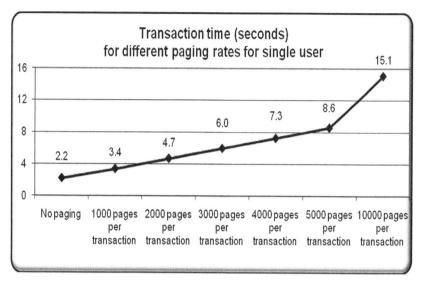

Chart 6.7.   Paging causes degradation of transaction time for single user.

operations have to be executed to process one transaction. If the size of one page is exactly 10 KB, then 1000 pages have to be delivered to memory from the disk to satisfy one request.

We solve the model in Fig. 6.3 for different paging rates for 100, 200, and 300 users. The model's workload and transaction profile are specified in Table 6.2. To read one page, the I/O controller works 0.03 sec and the disk works 0.1 sec.

The first model deliverable is the transaction time for a single user for different paging rates (Chart 6.7). Paging impact on transaction time is dramatic—it might increase transaction time manifold; on our chart it went from 2.2 sec to 15.1 sec when the paging rate was increased from 0 to 10,000 pages per transaction. We have to underscore that this is a raise that happened for a single user in a system without any queues.

Time degradation is more striking when the number of users increases (Chart 6.8). Under a higher paging rate, the system can serve fewer users without a negative impact on response time. For example, for 100 users, response time degradation starts when the paging rate exceeds 5,000 pages per transaction, but for 300 users, it occurs at a much smaller rate of 3,000 pages per transaction.

Paging leads to lower CPU utilization (Chart 6.9); for 300 users it went down from almost 100% to 33%.

Table 6.2
Workload and Transaction Profile for the Paging Model

Workload			Transaction Profile				
					Disk Access Time		
Transaction Name	Number of Users	Transaction Rate	Time in Node "Network"	Time in Node "CPUs"	Time in Node "Controller"	Time in Node "Disks"	Number of Pages Transferred Per Transaction
Interactive transactions	100, 200, 300	15	0.05 sec	2 sec	0.03 sec	0.1 sec	1,000, 2,000, 3,000, 4,000, 5,000, 10,000

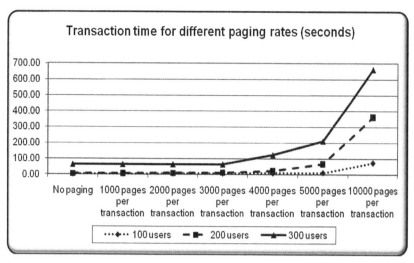

Chart 6.8. Paging causes a steep degradation of transaction time for multiple users.

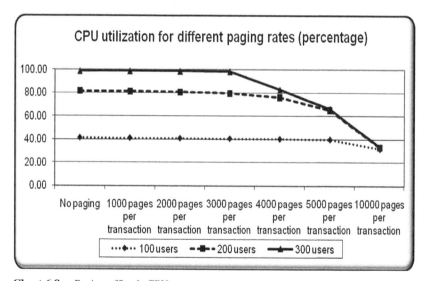

Chart 6.9. Paging offloads CPUs.

At the same time, paging has just the opposite effect on an I/O system. Charts 6.10 and 6.11 demonstrate that a disk is loaded at more than 80%, and the I/O system controller reaches its maximum capacity.

It has to be noted that depending on a device's speed, a disk can be maxed out but not the I/O system controller as it is in our example;

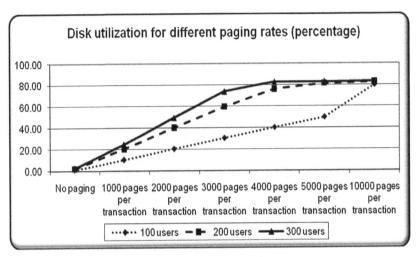

Chart 6.10.   Growing paging substantially loads the disk.

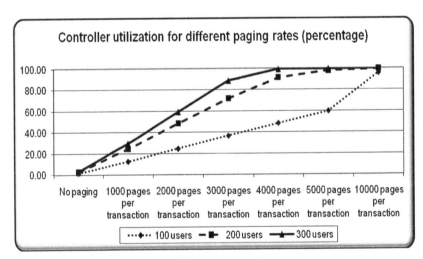

Chart 6.11.   Paging maxes out the I/O system controller.

the main conclusion here is that paging loads components of the I/O system and offloads CPUs.

Research of the paging model lets us put together the guidelines for identifying memory bottlenecks due to paging:

- Set up monitoring of memory paging, making sure you monitor so-called hard page faults, which happen when there are I/O operations. Some monitoring tools also include in page faults "soft page faults," which do not require an I/O transaction because the needed data are found somewhere in memory.

- Compare paging when the system is idle vs. the system with active users. Memory paging due to users' activity can be qualified as significant only in relative terms.

- Generate an increasing load using load generation tools or monitor production system under workloads with different intensities.

- Memory bottleneck due to paging is present if, as workload increases: (1) the paging rate grows and then flattens out; (2) CPU utilization goes down; (3) I/O system utilization is reaching its maximum (either disks or controllers).

Paging bottlenecks can be resolved by increasing memory size; they also can be addressed by scaling the I/O system.

Take Away from the Memory Bottleneck Model

- *To identify a bottleneck that is due to a preset application upper memory limit we have to monitor the system over a period of time when the number of users is increasing. A bottleneck is present if the following conditions are observed as the number of users grows: (1) memory allocated to the application has reached its upper limit; (2) hardware is underutilized; (3) transaction response time is getting longer.*

- *To identify a bottleneck that is due to paging we have to monitor the system over a period of time when the number of users is increasing. A bottleneck is present if the following conditions are observed as the number of user grows: (1) the paging rate grows and then flattens out; (2) utilization of hardware components except the I/O system goes down; (3) the I/O system utilization reaches its maximum.*

- *When identifying a paging bottleneck, make sure to monitor "hard page faults" that count transactions with the disk and do not count pages retrieved from memory.*

- *Increasing an application's memory size can resolve a bottleneck that is due to limited memory.*

- *A paging bottleneck can be resolved by increasing memory size; it also can be fixed by scaling the I/O system.*

6.3. THREAD OPTIMIZATION

A software thread is a sequence of an application's code statements that are executed one by one by a CPU. A single-threaded application can use only one CPU; a multithreaded application is able to create a few concurrent code flows and to load a few CPUs at the same time (Fig. 6.4).

A single-threaded application serving requests from interactive users is capable of processing all of them in timely manner using one CPU if the rate of requests is low. But under an intense workload, one CPU will be maxed out and the other ones will stay idle because the application cannot create additional streams of code.

Multithreaded applications parallelize processing of incoming requests (be it from users or large batch tasks) and are capable of using concurrently different hardware components (CPUs, servers, I/O subsystems) and by the same token increasing system throughput. Multithreaded applications implement two kinds of parallelization:

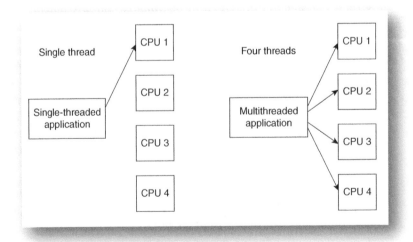

Figure 6.4.   Single-threaded and multithreaded applications.

- Serving concurrently multiple transactions initiated by different users.
- Breaking down a single transaction into multiple independent tasks. In that case, two techniques are in play (we analyze both in Chapter 9):
  - Concurrent transaction processing by a few servers.
  - Concurrent transaction processing by a few CPUs or by a CPU and an I/O subsystem of the same server.

The OS keeps an account of software threads spawned by the applications and allocates a CPU to a waiting thread for a particular time slice; after slice expiration it checks all waiting threads and allocates a CPU to another one. Indeed, more OS time is needed as more threads are initiated by the applications. Finding an optimal thread number is critical for application performance: too few threads lead to underutilization of hardware; too many threads overstress the system because of the high system overhead associated with their management by OS.

The number of an application's threads is usually reported by monitoring tools as **Number of threads per process**. Each individual thread is characterized by a few counters; among them are **%Processor time per thread**, **%System time per thread**, **Thread state**, etc. Thread-related counters provide a variety of data that help to evaluate a thread's functionality and optimize the number of threads. As an example, if some threads are not using CPUs, they can be terminated to minimize system overhead.

Thread Optimization Models

Thread Bottleneck Identification

We embark on defining thread bottleneck identification methodology and use for our research the model in Fig. 6.3 that has two CPUs, one disk controller, and four disks. The workload, the transaction profile, as well as the number of threads allocated to the application are defined in Table 6.3. The number of threads is a variable parameter that has to be tuned in order to deliver the fastest transaction time.

The modeling results for the case when a single user request is processed on two threads are presented in Chart 6.12. Up to 200 users can be served by the system without noticeable degradation of response

Table 6.3
Input Data for the Thread Bottleneck Identification Model

Workload							
			Transaction Profile				
					Disk Access Time		
Transaction Name	Number of Users	Transaction Rate	Time in Node "Network"	Time in Node "CPUs"	Time in Node "Controller"	Time in Node "Disks"	Number of Threads Per Application
Interactive transactions	100, 200, 300	15	0.05 sec	2 sec	0.03 sec	0.1 sec	20

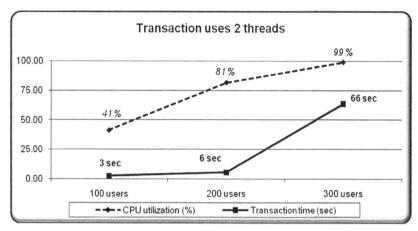

Chart 6.12. Transaction time and CPU utilization when a transaction uses two threads.

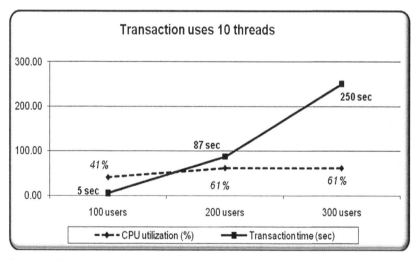

Chart 6.13. Transaction time and CPU utilization when a transaction uses 10 threads.

time; the CPU utilization for 200 users is still acceptable as it slightly exceeds 80%; for 300 users, CPUs are practically maxed out as they are running at 99% of capacity.

When one transaction needs 10 threads, a significant transaction time increase takes place for 200 and 300 users, and (this is an indication of a thread bottleneck) CPU utilization flattens out and CPUs stay underutilized (Chart 6.13).

A thread bottleneck offloads the I/O system in the same way it does for CPUs: If a program cannot be executed efficiently it definitely will generate fewer I/O operations. Actually, a thread bottleneck slows down the rate of requests from a program to all hardware components as well as to the OS.

A conducted study helps to lay down a methodology of thread bottleneck identification:

- Find out the number of threads for an application you are about to tune
- Measure response time and monitor utilization of hardware components
- Generate a growing load by using load generation tools or monitor the system under workloads with different intensities
- Monitor memory utilization and paging rate for the program
- Bottleneck due to insufficient number of threads is present if, as workload increases: (1) transaction time steeply grows; (2) the CPU and I/O systems are underutilized; (3) the application did not reach the upper memory limit; (4) paging rate is flat or even goes down

Correlation Among Transaction Time, CPU Utilization, and the Number of Threads

We use the model in Fig. 6.3 to analyze the relationship between transaction time and CPU utilization on the one hand and the number of an application's threads on the other. First, we consider a pure theoretical case that does not take into account OS overhead associated with thread management; the next study factors in the impact of management overhead.

The workload for the model is generated by 300 users; workload and transaction profile are defined in Table 6.4. We solve the model for a single-threaded application as well as when it spawns 10, 20, and 40 threads.

The model predicts that the single-threaded application delivers the longest transaction time (400 sec) and the lowest CPU utilization equal to 46% (Chart 6.14). A much-improved transaction time at 92 sec is delivered by the application with 20 threads. CPU utilization approaches 90% for 20 threads; further increase in the number of threads maxes out the CPUs.

Table 6.4
Workload and Transaction Profile for the Thread Bottleneck Model

Workload			Transaction Profile				
					Disk Access Time		
Transaction Name	Number of Users	Transaction Rate	Time in Node "Network"	Time in Node "CPUs"	Time in Node "Controller"	Time in Node "Disks"	Number of Threads Per Application
Interactive transactions	300	15	0.05 sec	2 sec	0.03 sec	0.1 sec	1, 10, 20, 30, 40

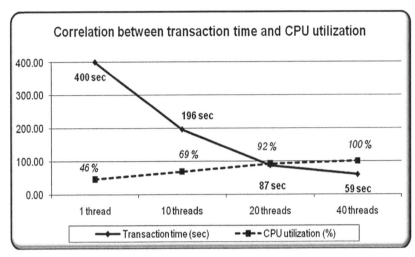

Chart 6.14. Transaction time and CPU utilization as functions of the number of threads (theoretical case without management overhead).

To conclude, in a theoretical case when thread management overhead does not exist, an increase in the number of threads completely eliminates any bottlenecks on the software level and enables maximum utilization of system hardware. The reality, sadly, is that everything has its price, and thread management does not come for free either. We will study its impact in the next section.

Optimal Number of Threads

As we learned in Chapter 5, a swelling system complexity drives up OS overhead. We will expand our model to factor in OS overhead due to the number of threads: In addition to input data per Table 6.4, we assume that each thread increases CPU time at 0.1 %, which accounts for OS system time. OS overhead is defined in Table 6.5.

Modeling results indicate that an optimal number of threads do exist, and they deliver the best response time (Chart 6.15). In our study, the optimum is reached at 40 threads; any further thread increase impedes system performance.

Tuning the number of threads is a two-step process. First we have to identify if a thread bottleneck is present by following the methodology discussed in the section *"Thread bottleneck identification."* Second, we optimize the number of threads to minimize response time.

Table 6.5
Time in Node CPUs for Different Numbers of Threads

Number of threads	10	20	40	100	200
% Increase in CPU time due to OS overhead	1%	2%	4%	10%	20%
Time in node "CPUs" (sec)	2.01	2.04	2.08	2.2	2.4

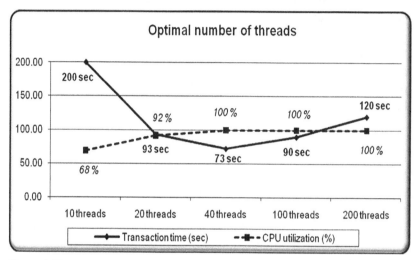

Chart 6.15.   Transaction time and CPU utilization for different numbers of threads (real case with management overhead).

Take Away from Thread Optimization Model

- *Bottleneck due to insufficient number of threads is present if, as workload increases: (1) transaction time sharply grows; (2) CPUs and I/O systems are underutilized; (3) the application does not reach its upper memory limit; (4) the paging rate is flat or even goes down.*

- *For a hypothetical system that does not have system overhead to manage threads, the model shows the possibility of eliminating a bottleneck by increasing the number of threads and by the same token minimizing transaction time.*

- *In a real system, thread management takes its share of system capacity and leads to an increase in transaction time after the number of threads has reached its optimal level.*

- *Thread optimization is a two-step process: first a thread bottleneck has to be identified; after that we have to start increasing the number of threads until a minimum transaction time is reached; any subsequent growth in the number of threads leads to a transaction time increase.*

6.4. OTHER CAUSES OF SOFTWARE BOTTLENECKS

We review a few other common causes of software bottlenecks; they are either relatively simple to interpret and so do not require building new models, or they can be analyzed by the models we already have built.

Transaction Affinity

Some applications limit the number of servers or CPUs a particular type of transaction can be processed on. For example (Fig. 6.5), in a three-server system, the reporting transactions can be processed only by two servers and the consolidation transactions only by one. Such an arrangement (called "transaction affinity") is similar to serving trucks and passenger cars by different tollbooths.

Transaction affinity divides total system capacity among different types of requests in order to make sure transactions do not compete for the same hardware resources. That does not prevent bottlenecks from happening. It is quite possible to have a bottleneck for a reporting transaction, while at the same time hardware allocated to consolidations is underutilized or even idle. To fix a reporting bottleneck we have to reallocate hardware resources, but reallocation can increase the probability of a consolidation bottleneck. To make the right decision regarding hardware allocation, the utilization of a system by different requests has to be monitored over a representative period of time.

Connections to Database; User Sessions

The impact of the number of database connections as well as user sessions on server utilization and transaction time is similar to the one produced by software threads. In a sense, database connections and user

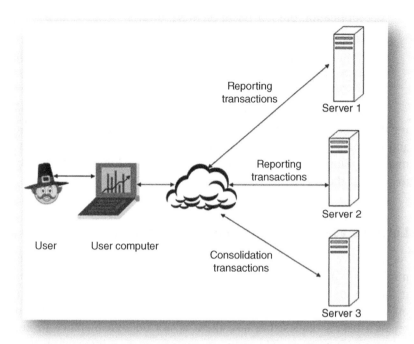

Figure 6.5. Transaction affinity.

sessions are similar to software threads—database connections enable concurrent access to the database; user sessions make it possible for a number of users to interact with a system concurrently. Each database connection and user session requires OS time to be managed; a performance gain due to an increase in the number of connections or sessions after some threshold will be outweighed by a rising OS overhead. As in the case of software threads, there are optimal numbers of database connections and user sessions.

Identification of the bottlenecks caused by inadequate numbers of database connections or user sessions is similar to the software thread jam detection we have discussed in this chapter. The matter can be dramatically complicated if the system has an insufficient number of all three parameters: software threads, database connections, and user sessions.

Below are a few signs that software has a shortage of one, two, or all of the above resources and is not capable of generating enough concurrent requests to keep the available hardware fully utilized:

1. Application did not reach memory limit
2. Utilization of hardware components (CPUs and I/O) is low
3. Transaction time grows exponentially after the number of users reached some threshold

The optimal value of each of the parameters can be found by changing them one at a time and monitoring the effect on hardware utilization and response time; this process can be time consuming as it requires many iterations. Methodologies we have discussed in this chapter help to conduct the process efficiently.

Limited Wait Time and Limited Wait Space

As we have learned, any request while traveling across a system might wait in queues until the needed service is provided. Waiting in queues extends response time, and some systems impose a limit on wait time if it exceeds a user's comfort threshold. Other systems reject a user's request because there is not enough memory to keep it in a waiting queue. Those two types of negative impacts on transaction time happen because of unsatisfactory system performance and can be considered bottlenecks because they are the results of slow processing, which leads to the expiration of wait time or a shortage of wait space.

Systems with limited wait time return a time-out message to a user when a limit is reached; such a message is a very articulate indication of a bottleneck. The good news about a limited wait time is that that kind of bottlenecks is self-identifiable as it generates an alarm when happening; the bad news is that identification of a bottleneck's causes and their remediation is still business as usual.

Systems with limited wait space enforce such restrictions when the transaction requires the handling of a large volume of data, and the data have to be loaded into memory in order to enable fast processing. A limited wait space bottleneck can be fixed by lowering the software parameter that defines space size, but a drawback is that the application will request memory a few times as it has to process a volume of data that exceeds the allocated memory size, and, in turn, will make the transaction time longer.

Software Locks

Multithreaded applications have to deal with a fairly complex policy of handling access to resources in a way that ensures proper synchronization and preserves data integrity. Here is a representative situation: a few managers are submitting data on the number of new wireless phone company contacts signed and approved during the past few hours; each manager does it for a different city located in New York State. After the data have been accepted from one manager, information for all of New York State has to be recalculated, and for that period of time the application is locked and blocks input from all other managers; their requests have to wait till the lock is released. The impact of a lock on transaction time in this case is obvious. Moreover, lock management requires OS attention and that is always associated with overhead. If thousands of managers have access to the application (which is not an overstatement for a large phone company), then the probability of locking is high, and its impact on performance could be unacceptable. The negative impact of software locks has to be evaluated by testing the application before releasing it into production; if impacts are present, there are usually two ways to alleviate them: either by redesigning the software algorithms or by changing the data structure. Unfortunately, both undertakings are time consuming and expensive. What would be welcome developments in that area are tunable locking algorithms that expose parameters that performance engineers can change and fix the bottleneck.

TAKE AWAY FROM THE CHAPTER

- *Software bottlenecks prevent an application from using all available hardware resources even if there is a demand for them. They are caused by either the settings of the application tuning parameters or by application design deficiencies.*

- *Multithreading is a prevailing design pattern of enterprise applications because it enables the application to use concurrent processing in different instances:*
  - *Accepting and serving request from many users*
  - *Accessing databases over multiple connections*

- *Taking advantage of multiple CPUs and cores by processing simultaneously the number of transactions initiated by different users as well as by parallelizing single transactions*
- *Implementing I/O operations in parallel with processing in CPUs*

Guidance on multithreading programming techniques for multi-core and hyper-threaded hardware architecture can be found in Herlihy and Shavit [6.1], Duffy [6.2], and Breshears [6.3].

- *To identify a bottleneck that is due to a preset application upper memory limit we have to monitor the system over a period of time when the number of users is increasing. A bottleneck is present if the following conditions are observed as the number of users grows: (1) memory allocated to the application has reached an upper limit; (2) hardware is underutilized; (3) transaction response time is getting longer.*
- *To identify a bottleneck that is due to paging, we have to monitor the system over a period of time when the number of users is increasing. A bottleneck is present if the following conditions are observed as the number of users grows: (1) paging rate grows and then flattens out; (2) utilization of hardware components except the I/O system goes down; (3) I/O system utilization reaches maximum.*
- *A bottleneck due to an insufficient number of threads is present if, as workload increases: (1) transaction time sharply grows; (2) CPUs and I/O systems are underutilized; (3) the application did not reach its upper memory limit; (4) paging rate is flat or even goes down.*
- *Thread optimization is a two-step process: first, a thread bottleneck has to be identified; after that we have to start increasing the number of threads until a minimum transaction time is reached; any subsequent growth in the number of threads leads to transaction time increase.*

## CHAPTER 7

Performance and Capacity of Virtual Systems

In this chapter: what is virtualization; virtualization performance penalty; methodology of virtual machine sizing.

7.1. WHAT IS VIRTUALIZATION?

The use of a virtualization paradigm is on the rise, and prevailing enthusiasm often shields coupled performance punishments imposed on some applications. An analysis of the impact of virtualization on performance helps to determine the applications suitable for deployment on virtual platforms as well as the appropriate platform size.

Virtualization in the realm of computer systems is a trickery achieved by an abstraction software layer that separates an application from its underlying hardware and software in order to provide functional and cost-related advantages. An abstraction software layer can be located on any of three levels of a system stack. It can be placed between the hardware and the OS; in such a case, an application is

Solving Enterprise Applications Performance Puzzles: Queuing Models to the Rescue,
First Edition. Leonid Grinshpan.
© 2012 Institute of Electrical and Electronics Engineers. Published 2012 by John Wiley
& Sons, Inc.

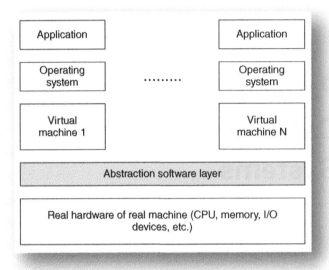

Figure 7.1. Virtualization by dividing hardware resources.

running on a subset of hardware available on a physical platform, mostly on a limited number of CPUs and limited memory size (Fig. 7.1). Virtual machines are called "guests," and a real machine is called a "host."

If the abstraction layer is located between the OS and the application, it gives the application portability among different OSs (Fig. 7.2).

An abstraction layer can be implemented as a high-level programming language virtual machine—the best known example is the Java virtual machine (Fig. 7.3).

What is common among all virtualization technologies is that they introduce an additional software layer into a system, and that obviously has a degrading impact on performance. The scope of such an impact varies depending on implementation of abstraction layers. Factoring into a model an overhead generated by the abstraction software layer can be done the same way as taking into account OS overhead (Chapter 5).

Virtualization is enabled by additional software layers that impact system performance in the same way an OS does.

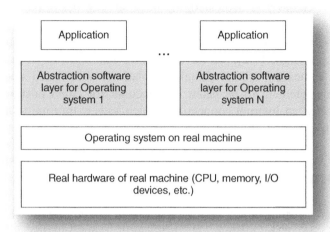

Figure 7.2. Virtualization by making an application OS independent.

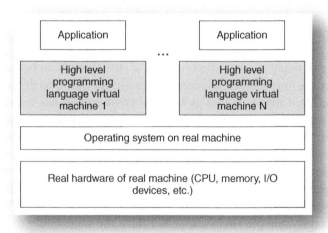

Figure 7.3. Virtualization by programming language virtual machine.

By some estimates (for example, by Thompson Reuters Elite business http://www.elite.com/virtualization_servers/) CPU overhead reduces performance by 15–20% or more in some cases, and disk I/O sequential read performance degrades by 15–70% depending on architecture. Interesting considerations of virtualization overhead can be found in Salsburg [7.1].

This chapter is dedicated to the study of performance-related aspects of hardware virtualization, a very popular technology with an extensive presence that also represents a backbone of the cloud computing paradigm [7.2]. Cloud computing features the same performance demeanor as the virtualized platform it is build upon; one additional element to be taken into account for cloud hosting is the presence of an Internet connection, which adds extra time to the total transaction time.

7.2. HARDWARE VIRTUALIZATION

Hardware virtualization can be compared to cutting a whole pie into pieces. This analogy is sufficiently representative with two exceptions.

Firstly, it is impossible to divide some hardware components among virtual machines; they will always be shared. An obvious reason: A single component cannot be shared. The examples of commonly used components are memory bus, motherboard bus, external ports, I/O system controller, and floating-point unit. Components that are not shared will delay request processing by a virtual machine because they limit access to resources assigned to the virtual machine. In modeling terms, all that means is that any virtual environment has a number of nodes that process incoming requests from the applications that reside on different virtual machines, and they might create congestion on those nodes. Applications with intense usage of components that are not shared components (for example, an I/O system or floating-point unit) might suffer a great deal of performance loss if they are deployed on a virtual platform.

Secondly, the pie slices altogether have the same count of calories as a whole pie, whereas *the total capacity of all guest virtual machines is lower than the total capacity of the non-virtualized host server*. That means that the virtualization's performance penalty is due not only to additional software layers and congestion on components that are not shared, but to a much higher degree to lower server capacity. A practical suggestion is that only applications with low-resource-demanding workloads are good candidates to be moved over to virtual machines because the maintenance-related cost advantage will outweigh performance loss. That is not the case for the enterprise applications with respectable appetite for capacity and we will resort to modeling to research that.

The total capacity of all guest virtual machines is lower than the total capacity of the non-virtualized host server.

Non-Virtualized Hosts

We begin our analysis by modeling a non-virtual platform supporting, for example, a private cloud deployed within a corporation. No matter what kind of hardware a cloud is built upon, as well as how it might be broken down by virtual machines, a cloud always has a finite capacity shared among diversified applications. That means the workloads from disparate applications are in a competition for limited resources; redistribution of cloud resources to satisfy fluctuations of one workload might impact the performance of some or all other workloads. In order to account for such specifics, a cloud model has to have multiple "User" nodes representing users of different applications. Figure 7.4 presents a model of a cloud serving two applications.

Node "Users A" stands for the users of Application A; node "Users B" corresponds to the users of Application B. Users of each application

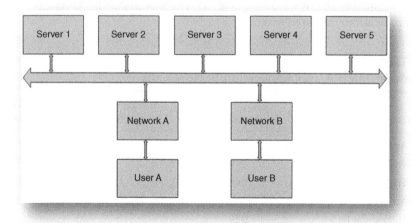

Figure 7.4. Model of a non-virtualized cloud with two applications.

access the cloud's servers over different networks represented by the nodes "Network A" and "Network B." Overall, the cloud's hardware capacity is characterized by five nodes "Server 1" to "Server 5," each one having eight CPUs. Because assignment of the servers to applications is highly dynamic we refrain from using more descriptive identifications such as "Web server," "Database server," etc. (being virtualized, the same server might have two virtual machines: one hosts the database for Application A, and another hosts the Web component for Application B).

At any given time for each server, a cloud provider has to know what percentage of a server's capacity is consumed by each workload as well as the percentage of unused capacity; those data can be obtained by monitoring. It is a matter of success or failure for a cloud provider to have the estimates of such percentages for future workload fluctuations as they let the provider reallocate resources in a timely manner that will satisfy a workload's ups and downs. This is where no other tool or technology can be as helpful as a model.

Let's assume Application A's workload consists of Transaction A1 and Transaction A2; Application B's workload includes Transaction B1 and Transaction B2. The definitions of both workloads are in the Table 7.1.

Transaction profiles for both workloads are described in Table 7.2.

We excluded from the profiles the times in Networks A and B, assuming for simplicity that they are very small and can be ignored. Transaction profiles indicate that we evaluate the deployment of two applications on three servers.

Table 7.1
Application A and Application B Workloads

Transaction Name	Number of Users	Average Number of Transactions Per User Per Hour
Application A Workload		
Transaction A1	50	10
Transaction A2	100	5
Application B Workload		
Transaction B1	200	20
Transaction B2	300	10

Table 7.2

Transaction Profiles for Applications A and B

	Server 1	Server 2	Server 3	Server 4	Server 5
Application A					
Transaction A1	1 sec	4 sec	1 sec	0	0
Transaction A2	0.5 sec	3 sec	0.5 sec	0	0
Application B					
Transaction B1	1 sec	2 sec	0.5 sec	0	0
Transaction B2	1 sec	2 sec	1 sec	0	0

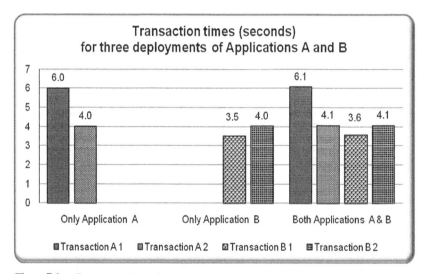

Chart 7.1. Transaction times for three deployments of Applications A and B.

We analyzed the model for three scenarios: only Application A is deployed; only Application B is deployed; both Application A and Application B are deployed.

Per the modeling results on Chart 7.1 we can conclude that both applications can comfortably coexist on Servers 1, 2, and 3 as the impact on transaction times is practically nonexistent.

Chart 7.2 shows the percentage of server utilization by each application; we can see that Application B is much more demanding than Application A. We also can see substantial headroom on Servers 1

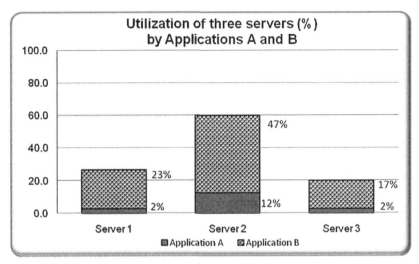

Chart 7.2. Percentage of server utilizations by Applications A and B.

Table 7.3
Transaction Profiles for Redeployed Applications A and B

	Server 1	Server 2	Server 3	Server 4	Server 5
Application A					
Transaction A1	2 sec	4 sec	0	0	0
Transaction A2	1 sec	3 sec	0	0	0
Application B					
Transaction B1	1.5 sec	2 sec	0	0	0
Transaction B2	2 sec	2 sec	0	0	0

and 3, which suggests that Applications A and B can be redeployed to free up one server.

Let's check performance and resource consumption when applications are hosted on two servers. Transaction profiles for redeployed applications are presented in Table 7.3.

Chart 7.3 shows how redeployed applications utilize Servers 1 and 2.

The model confirms that transaction times are practically unchanged. We can conclude that hosting both applications on two servers is acceptable from a performance standpoint as it minimizes the number of physical servers and does not increase transaction time.

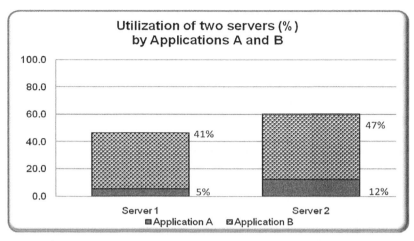

Chart 7.3. Percentage of server utilizations when Applications A and B are hosted on two servers.

Virtualized Hosts

We want to isolate the applications by setting up two virtual machines on each server: one machine for Application A and the second one for Application B. Servers 1 and 2 have eight CPUs each, and we have to find out how many CPUs should be assigned to each virtual machine.

To begin with, let's establish a correspondence between server utilization and the number of CPUs in use. Servers 1 and 2 have eight CPUs each, and 100% of server utilization indicates that all eight CPUs are busy; that means each busy CPU contributes 12.5% to total server utilization (100%/8 CPUs = 12.5%). As an example, if total server utilization is 25%, then two CPUs are processing workloads.

The modeling results in Table 7.4 show the utilization of non-partitioned Servers 1 and 2 by Applications A and B and the corresponding number of CPUs.

Let's find out what performance can deliver virtual machines with the numbers of CPUs according to Table 7.4 (in the following discussion we are using designations of virtual machines as shown in Table 7.5).

The answer can be found by solving the models for Applications A and B deployed on dedicated virtual machines (Fig. 7.5). The model's outputs indicate significant response time degradations for both applications on virtual platforms vs. non-partitioned deployment (Table 7.6).

Table 7.4
Distribution of CPUs Between Applications A and B

		Application A	Application B
Server 1	Utilization	5.5%	41%
	Number of CPUs	1	4
Server 2	Utilization	12%	47.8%
	Number of CPUs	1	4

Table 7.5
Distribution of CPU Between Virtual Machines

	Virtual Machines for Application A	Virtual Machines for Application B
Server 1	VM A1 (1 CPU)	VM B1 (4 CPU)
Server 2	VM A2 (1 CPU)	VM B2 (4 CPU)

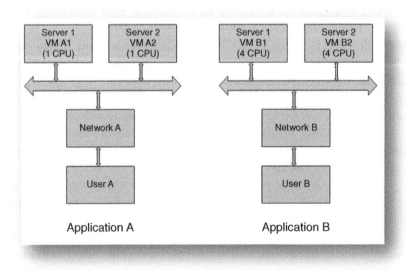

Figure 7.5. Model of the deployments of Applications A and B on virtual machines.

Table 7.6

Transaction Response Time for Non-Virtual and Virtual
Application Deployments

	Application A Deployment Platform		Application B Deployment Platform	
	Non-Virtual	Virtual	Non-Virtual	Virtual
Transaction A1	6.0 sec	34.4 sec	N/A	N/A
Transaction A2	4.0 sec	34.6 sec	N/A	N/A
Transaction B1	N/A	N/A	3.5 sec	9.5 sec
Transaction B1	N/A	N/A	4.0 sec	10.0 sec

Table 7.7

System CPUs Utilization for Non-Virtual and Virtual
Application Deployments

Application A Deployment Platform				Application B Deployment Platform			
Server 1	VM A1	Server 2	VM A2	Server 1	VM B1	Server 2	VM B2
5.2%	38.0%	12.0%	90.0%	41.0%	80.0%	47.8%	93.0%

The roots of performance disappointment can be found in CPU utilization of virtual machines VM A2 and VM B2—they are too high (90% and above) to deliver acceptable transaction times (Table 7.7).

The explanation of the modeling results requires a short foray into queuing theory. Let's take a deep breath and dive in . . .

Queuing Theory Explains It All

For the purpose of our analysis it is sufficient to consider only one eight-CPU physical server from the non-virtualized host model pictured in Fig. 7.5. As we extract it from the queuing network, we have to take into account the incoming and outgoing flow of requests represented by the arrows in Fig. 7.6. We partition the physical server into eight virtual machines with a single CPU each, and we compare eight processing units model of a physical server with one processing unit model of a virtual machine.

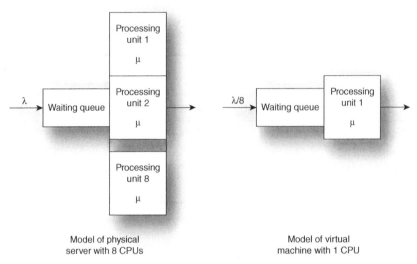

Model of physical
server with 8 CPUs

Model of virtual
machine with 1 CPU

Figure 7.6. Models of a physical server and a virtual machine.

The transactions come into the physical server with a rate λ *requests/ second*; the incoming transaction rate for the virtual machine is eight times lower because as we break the physical server into eight virtual machines, we direct only one-eighth of incoming transactions to each virtual machine. One processing unit of each model is capable of serving μ *requests/second*.

We are using queuing theory's Little's formula to calculate response time for both models assuming that $\lambda = 16$ *requests/second* and $\mu = 4$ *requests/second*.

The response time for the nondivided physical server is:

$$T(physical) = 1/(\mu - \lambda) = 1/(4*8-16) = 0.0625 \ sec.$$

The response time for the virtual machine is:

$$T(virtual) = 1/(\mu - \lambda/8) = 1/(4-2) = 0.5 \ sec.$$

Response time degradation is due to a longer waiting time $W(virtual)$ in the virtual machine queue as opposed to the waiting time $W(physical)$ in the physical server queue:

$$W(physical) = (1/(\mu - \lambda)) - 1/\mu*8 = 0.0625 - 1/4*8 = 0.03125 \ sec.$$
$$W(virtual) = 1/(\mu - \lambda/8) - 1/\mu = 0.5 - 1/4 = 0.25 \ sec.$$

This theoretical result at first might be striking, but it will not be much of a surprise if we refresh our memory of the behavior of queues in two real-life environments: the toll plaza and the movie theater box office.

A toll plaza with booths that are equally accessible by any car has lower congestion than the same plaza with booths divided by two categories: ones serving only sedans and the others serving only trucks. An intuitive explanation is that in the nondivided plaza, in the absence of trucks, a sedan can be processed by any booth and vice versa; in a divided plaza, the booths dedicated to trucks will stay idle even if there is a queue of sedans. The same behavior is exhibited by the queues in a box office—if any window serves any theatergoer, then the waiting queue is not as long as in the case when some windows serve only particular customer categories.

We have to note that in our model of a physical server, all processing units have the same capacity, μ *requests/second*, which means that the total capacity of a node with eight processing units accounts for 8μ *requests/second*. In a real physical server, an increase in the number of CPUs N times does not make server N times more productive because of growing management overhead. For that reason, partitioning a physical server will bring down its capacity a little less dramatically (if that can be of any consolation).

At this point, we are armed with important knowledge of physical machine partition performance implications, and we can find out the right sizes for the virtual machines for Applications A and B.

Virtualized Hosts Sizing After Lesson Learned

We start sizing virtual machines according to Table 7.8 (two CPUs on each virtual machine hosting Application A, and six CPUs on each virtual machine hosting Application B).

Table 7.8
Distribution of CPUs Between Virtual Machines

	Virtual Machines for Application A	Virtual Machines for Application B
Server 1	VM A1 (2 CPU)	VM B1 (6 CPU)
Server 2	VM A2 (2 CPU)	VM B2 (6 CPU)

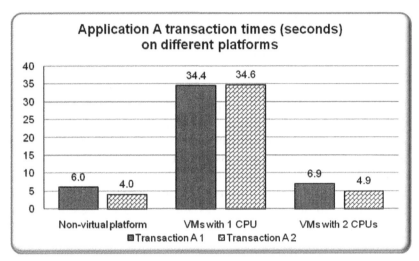

Chart 7.4. Performance of Application A on different platforms.

Table 7.9
Number of CPUs for Each Application for Non-Virtual and
Virtual Platforms

	Application A Deployment Platform		Application B Deployment Platform	
	Non-Virtual	Virtual	Non-Virtual	Virtual
Server 1	1	2	4	6
Server 2	1	2	4	6

The model's estimates for Application A on all platforms are shown in Chart 7.4. Deployment of Application A on a non-virtual platform delivers the shortest transaction times. A one-CPU virtual machine provides terrible performance. Setup with two CPUs per virtual machine increases transaction time 15–22%.

To conclude, private cloud analysis showed that Applications A and B can be supported with more or less acceptable degradation in transaction time by partitioning each eight-CPU physical server into two virtual machines—one with two CPUs and a second one with six CPUs.

Table 7.9 compares the number of CPUs providing adequate performance levels for Applications A and B on virtual and non-virtual

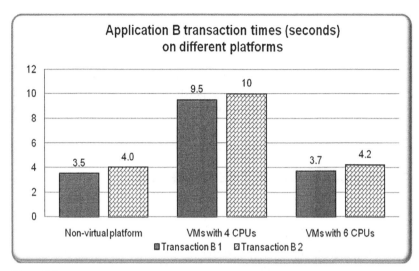

Chart 7.5. Performance of Application B on different platforms.

platforms. It can be seen that in order to avoid virtualization performance penalty we have to allocate additional CPUs to the virtual machines.

7.3. METHODOLOGY OF VIRTUAL MACHINES SIZING

The analysis of virtualization performance implications carried out in this chapter makes it possible to lay out a **methodology of virtual machines sizing.** The highlights of the methodology are:

1. Estimate capacity demand from each application either by monitoring the production system under realistic workloads or by using queuing models.
2. Analyze a few what-if scenarios to find out the minimal number of non-virtualized physical servers capable of supporting all applications and meeting service level requirements.
3. Identify the number of CPUs in use by each application based on non-virtualized server utilizations by each application. (For a server with N CPUs, one CPU contributes $100\%/N$ percent to

total utilization. If an application consumes $U\%$ of total server capacity, then the number of CPUs utilized by the application is $(U\%*N)/100\%$).

4. Allocate additional CPUs to each virtual machine to avoid performance degradation when partitioning a physical platform. An estimate of the number of CPUs can be provided by queuing models.

TAKE AWAY FROM THE CHAPTER

- *Virtualization's performance penalty is due to:*
  - *Additional software layers*
  - *Congestions on non-shared hardware components (memory bus, floating-point unit, etc.)*
  - *Loss of physical server capacity (the total capacity of all guest virtual machines is lower than the total capacity of the non-virtualized host server)*
- *Consolidation of applications on a virtual platform makes sense only when maintenance-related cost advantages prevail over performance loss.*
- *The devised methodology of virtual machine sizing lets us avoid performance degradation when partitioning the physical platform.*

## CHAPTER 8

Model-Based Application Sizing: Say Good-Bye to Guessing

In this chapter: why we need models for sizing; a model's input data; mapping an application into a model; analyzing what-if scenarios.

8.1. WHY MODEL-BASED SIZING?

Enterprise application deployment starts with system sizing—an evaluation of the number and capacity of hardware servers and appliances needed to ensure that an application will provide the expected level of service to business users. System sizing is of the utmost importance not just because it guarantees acceptable performance of application production deployment, but also because it helps to allocate the right budget for hardware and software procurement, installation, and maintenance.

The state of the matter is that the great majority of sizing estimates are provided without scientific analysis and are based on prior experience acquired from similar systems. The problem with the empirical approach to sizing is that as humans we tend to extrapolate linearly. Here are two examples of linear extrapolation:

Solving Enterprise Applications Performance Puzzles: Queuing Models to the Rescue,
First Edition. Leonid Grinshpan.
© 2012 Institute of Electrical and Electronics Engineers. Published 2012 by John Wiley
& Sons, Inc.

Table 8.1
Workload for Quiz 1

Transaction Name	Number of Users	Number of Transactions Per User Per Hour
Ticket Reservation (TR)	250	6

Example 1. If a server is running at 40–45% of its CPU capacity under a workload from 100 users, it will be running at 80–90% of its CPU capacity for 200 users.

Example 2. Doubling a number of CPUs in a server allows it to process twice as many requests.

To demonstrate how our linear thinking collides with reality we have devised a few quizzes:

Quiz 1. A ticket reservation application is deployed on one server with eight CPUs. The system is capable of delivering a 10-sec response time for a ticket reservation transaction under the workload described in Table 8.1.

Server monitoring showed that its total CPU utilization is 50% under the load from 250 users. Question: How many users can the application support without compromising response time? The answer obtained from the application's model is presented in Chart 8.1.

The model predicts that the application is capable of serving 350 users with a response time degradation under 10%. We would be entirely wrong in assuming that the system can support twice as many users; for 500 users, transaction time jumps exponentially up to 43 sec.

Quiz 2. In Quiz 1, a server was running at 50% of its capacity. Let's use the server's spare capacity and deploy another application that supports online payments. We want to estimate how many users our online payment system can serve so that it delivers a transaction time of 8 sec if each user submits 10 transactions per hour. The workload is specified in Table 8.2.

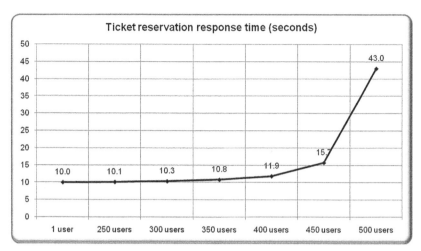

Chart 8.1.   Ticket reservation response time for different numbers of users.

Table 8.2
Workload for Quiz 2

Transaction Name	Number of Users	Number of Transactions Per User Per Hour
Ticket Reservation (TR)	250	6
Online Payment (OLP)	?	10

The modeling estimate can be seen in Chart 8.2. The model predicts that as soon as the number of online payment users reaches 100 there is a noticeable degradation of response time, not only for online payment transactions, but for ticket reservation transactions as well. It is unlikely for us to come to such a conclusion empirically.

Quiz 3. An enterprise application supporting financial consolidations for a large corporation has to process the workload defined in Table 8.3 and deliver a transaction time of 300 sec.

The corporation is using eight-way servers. The question is: How many servers have to be procured? The modeling prediction for one server is in Chart 8.3.

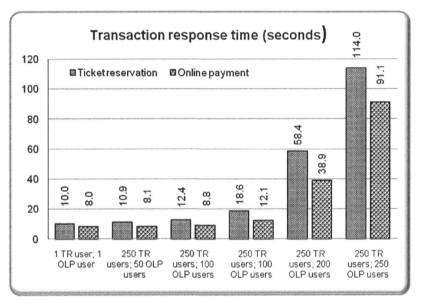

Chart 8.2. Ticket reservation and online payment transaction times for different numbers of users.

Table 8.3
Workload for Quiz 3

Transaction Name	Number of Users	Number of Transactions Per User Per Hour
Financial consolidation	150	2

The model forecasts that one server is capable of processing requests from 30 users; for a higher number of users, consolidation time goes well beyond 300 sec. That means five servers are needed to ensure an acceptable service level to 150 users. How close have you been to that prediction?

As we have seen, enterprise applications are nonlinear systems featuring exponential-like explosions of transaction times. The explosions are due to the queues, and queues are due to the system's finite resources, which are incapable of immediately satisfying all incoming requests. Even if an application has just two users, there is a nonzero probability that a transaction initiated by one user will need a resource

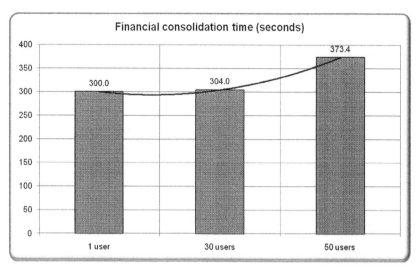

Chart 8.3.   Time of consolidation for different number of users.

taken by a transaction initiated by another user, and the second transaction will have to wait until the resource is released. Queuing models take into account queues and provide much better estimates than any empirical forecasts.

Model-based application sizing includes the following steps, discussed in detail in this chapter:

- Specification of model's input data (workload, transaction profile, hardware platform)
- Building model
- Solving model
- Analysis modeling results
- Analysis of different what-if scenarios

8.2. A MODEL'S INPUT DATA

Workload and Expected Transaction Time

A model-based sizing project requires specification of the model's input data. We have learned in the previous chapters that workload and transaction profiles have to be defined to solve a model. Workload characterization can be found either in SLA or by interviewing business users.

This is what we need for capacity planning:

1. A list of transactions
2. The number of users per each transaction
3. For each transaction, the anticipated number of transactions per user per hour (transaction rate)
4. For each transaction, the response time expected by the application users

We are familiar with the parameters 1–3 as we have used them in the previous chapters. Parameter 4 is a new one; it specifies an expected transaction response time, and usually it is defined by the business users. That time is specified when a single user is working with the application (no queues in a system).

Expected transaction response time is stated by the users based on their comfort level; users consider a system to be performing well if the time to process a transaction does not exceed an expected time. It is specified when a single user is working with the application.

As required by SLA, expected transaction time has to be met at the application deployment stage, when numerous application functions get implemented. An enterprise application, unlike off-the-shelf software, represents a collection of building blocks enabling very rich functionality; at the deployment stage that functionality is customized and aligned with a corporation's business data, practice, and policy. Application customization is a design process and during that process, a design team has to ensure that expected transaction response time is met for a single user. For the next step, appropriate application sizing ensures that the expected transaction time is delivered by the application when it is in use by many users.

If business users work in different geographical locations, parameters 1–4 have to be specified for each location. Table 8.4 is an example of a workload and expected transaction times for an application serving remote offices.

Table 8.4
Workload and Expected Transaction Time

Workload

Transaction Name	Number of Users	Number of Transactions Per User Per Hour	Expected Transaction Time
New York Users			
Consolidation A	10	2	300 sec
Consolidation B	30	5	60 sec
Report A	10	2	40 sec
Report B	30	5	20 sec
London Users			
Consolidation B	10	5	90 sec
Report B	10	5	30 sec
Hong Kong Users			
Report C	20	10	40 sec
Report D	15	5	30 sec

It can be seen that the users in New York expect to retrieve *Report B* in 20 sec, but the users in London have factored in network delay and expect *Report B* to be processed in 30 sec. The same realistic expectations are reflected in the response times for *Consolidation B*: it is 60 sec for New York users and 90 sec for London users.

How to Obtain a Transaction Profile

A transaction profile comprises the time intervals a transaction has spent in the system servers it has visited when the application was serving only a single request (no queues existed in any node). For the model in Fig. 8.1, a profile for transaction *Report ABC* (pictured as a sedan) includes times in the "Web," "Application," "Reports," and "Database" servers; a profile for transaction *Consolidation XYZ* (pictured as a truck) consists of the times in the "Web," "Application," "Consolidation," and "Database" servers.

Table 8.5 defines the profiles of transactions *Reports A, B, C* and *Consolidation XYZ*. The total of all components of the transaction profile is equal to the expected transaction time.

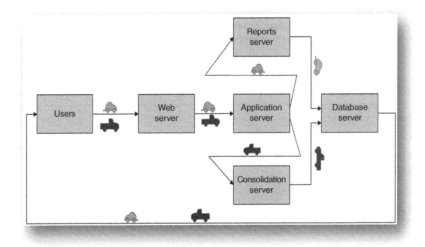

Figure 8.1. *Reports A, B, C* (sedans) and *Consolidation XYZ* (trucks) transactions.

If the application keeps in its logs the times of transactions process-ing on each hardware component, then we have readily available and reliable information on the transaction profile. The "Database server" always saves the time it spends to process queries; the "Web" and "Application" servers also maintain very informative logs. The chal-lenge might be to consolidate different records spread out in a number of logs in order to find the business transactions profiles; log file ana-lyzers make that process more efficient.

A transaction profile can be obtained by monitoring the utilization of system resources by that transaction. The rationale behind this approach is that while traveling across a system a transaction consumes system resources, and monitoring tools usually are capable of reporting how long each resource was busy serving a single transaction. We discussed in detail in Chapter 3 how to use monitors and utilities built into an OS for transaction profiling.

Chart 8.4 demonstrates the results of monitoring the "Application" and "Database" servers' utilizations during processing of a single trans-action. The X axis is time in seconds; the Y axis is utilization in percent-age points.

Table 8.5
Profiles of Transactions *Reports A, B, C* and *Consolidation XYZ*

Transaction Name	Time In Node "Web Server"	Time in Node "Application Server"	Time in Node "Reports Server"	Time in Node "Consolidation Server"	Time in Node "Database Server"	Expected Transaction Time
Reports A, B, C	1.0 sec	2.5 sec	7.0 sec	N/A	2.5 sec	13.0 sec
Consolidation XYZ	1.0 sec	2.0 sec	N/A	35.0 sec	8.0 sec	46.0 sec

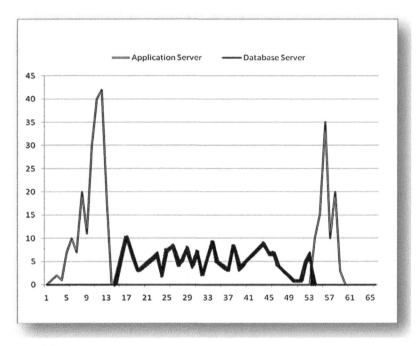

Chart 8.4. Utilization of the "Application" and "Database" servers.

For the first 15 sec, a transaction was processed by the "Application server" (gray thin line), then the transaction visited the "Database server" and spent 38 sec there (black thick line); finally, the transaction was served by the "Application server" for an additional 6 sec. Total transaction time is 59 seconds (21 sec in the "Application server" and 38 sec in "Database server").

Hardware Platform

To build a model we have to know the specifications of the hardware servers and appliances an application will be hosted on. The most important parameters of hardware for model-based sizing are the ones that determine the speed of transaction processing: CPU clock frequency, the number of CPUs, and various speed-impacting technologies like hyper-threading and multi-core CPUs. Because application sizing often includes a comparison of different hardware platforms, we need a numeric measure of the relative performance of diverse servers and appliances. Such metrics are obtained by running standardized software programs called benchmarks. Running the same benchmark on the servers from a variety of vendors sets a common playing field for measuring and comparison of a server's processing power.

Each benchmark emulates a workload designed to measure the performance of a specific hardware component or a function implemented by hardware. Here are a few of the most common areas of benchmarking: integer arithmetic, floating-point arithmetic, CPU and memory, I/O subsystem, server as a whole, system with multiple servers as a whole. Interpretation of benchmarking data requires an understanding of the variations between a benchmark-generated workload and an application workload. The closer a benchmark's workload is to the application's workload, the more representative the data will be for relative performance.

The best benchmark of a particular application is the application itself. Unfortunately, in real life it is only in rare circumstances that an enterprise application can be used as its own benchmark because of the very high cost of such a project. The engineering community must resort to a less expensive alternative based on industry-standard benchmarks that can be used (with the reasonable precautious) for different applications and hardware platforms. While identifying which benchmarking results to use for model-based sizing we have to ensure that the benchmark and its workload are similar to the ones for our application.

When sizing online transaction processing (OLTP) applications we can use standard benchmarks supported by the Transaction Processing Performance Council (TPC, www.tpc.org). The benchmark TPC-E simulates the workload generated by a brokerage firm, but the data structure, transactions, and implementation rules have been designed to be representative of a broad range of OLTP systems. The TPC-E benchmark measures performance of a central database that processes transactions; the benchmark delivers the number of transactions executed by the database in 1 sec (transactions per second [tps]). Relative performance of databases usually reported is shown in Table 8.6 (table entries are fictitious and only intended to give an idea of benchmark deliverables).

Using the tps metric we can evaluate the time of transaction processing by different databases. For example, in Table 8.6, the relative

Table 8.6

Relative Database Performance for TPC-E Benchmark

System	Tps	Processors		
		# of CPUs	# of Cores	# of Threads
SYSUNI 7020ES Model 670RP	2,000.78	16	64	128
ENCC Fire5800/A124	1,368.22	16	64	64
BMI System P x 3860 M56	1,845.00	16	64	64

performance of a SYSUNI system vs. an ENCC system is 2,000.78/1.368.22 = 1.46; that means if it is known that a transaction has spent 10 sec in the SYSUNI system, we can estimate that it will spend 6.85 sec in the ENCC system (10 sec/1.46 = 6.85 sec).

Another popular OLTP system benchmark is known as the TPC-C (www.tpc.org/tpcc); it mimics order-entry activities (entering orders, recording payments, checking order status, etc.). The benchmark is applicable to any applications that support management, sales, or distribution of the products or services. TPC-C also measures database performance in the number of transactions per second (tps).

Standard Performance Evaluation Corporation (SPEC, www.spec.org) maintains benchmarks that are applicable to a wide range of high-end computers and systems companies use to host enterprise applications. The SPEC CPU2006 benchmark primarily targets performance of a computer's CPUs and memory under a compute-intense workload. It includes two components: CINT2006 to measure integer arithmetic performance and CFP2006 to measure floating-point arithmetic performance. CPU2006 reports both metrics in normalized form using a reference computer to establish a baseline across all past and future benchmarking projects:

$$CPU\,2006\ metric =$$

$$\frac{Time\ to\ execute\ benchmark\ on\ reference\ computer}{Time\ to\ execute\ benchmark\ on\ tested\ computer}$$

For example, if on a reference system an execution of the CINT2006 benchmark takes 240 min and the same benchmark is executed on the tested computer for 10 min, then the normalized performance of the tested computer is 240/10 = 24.

SPEC maintains thousands of CPU2006 benchmarks. To find out the relative performance of different hardware systems you have to download a file with benchmarking results. The file lists hundreds of systems and contains the normalized performance of each one in a column named "Baseline." An example of data for the system Sun Fire X2270 is presented in Table 8.7.

The table indicates that the benchmark was executed on a Sun Fire X2270 with the particular type and number of CPUs, memory size, OS, and file system; that means relative performance metric takes into account main hardware and software specifications.

Table 8.7
CPU2006 Benchmark Results for Sun Fire X2270

Benchmark	CINT2006
Hardware vendor	Oracle Corporation
System	Sun Fire X2270 (Intel Xeon X5550 2.67GHz)
Baseline	**32**
# Cores	8
# Chips	2
# Cores per chip	4
# Threads per core	2
Processor	Intel Xeon X5550
Processor MHz	2667
Processor characteristics	Intel Turbo Boost Technology up to 3.06 GHz
1st level cache	32 KB I + 32 KB D on chip per core
2nd level cache	256 KB I + D on chip per core
3rd level cache	8 MB I + D on chip per chip
Other cache	None
Memory	24 GB (6 × 4 GB DDR3-1333)
Operating system	SuSe Linux SLES10 SP2
File system	ReiserFS

Here is an example of how to use the CPU2006 benchmark for model-based sizing. Let's assume we measured a transaction processing time on computer ABC and the time was 5 sec. We want to know the modeling predictions when the application is running on computer XYZ; as an input into the model we have to find out how long a transaction will be processed on computer XYZ. The CPU2006 benchmark has the speed metric for computer ABC equal to 35 and for computer XYZ it is 45. Relative performance is 45/35 = 1.28. That means that as the model's input data, we have to set the time on computer XYZ equal to 5/1.28 or 3.9 sec.

We discussed two industry-standard benchmarks; a uniqueness of a particular application might require special research to find out its relative performance for different hardware platforms. No matter how the relative speed metric is obtained, its usage is always the same as shown below:

transaction time on system 2 =

$$\text{transaction time on system } 1 * \frac{\text{relative performance of system } 1}{\text{relative performance of system } 2}$$

8.3. MAPPING A SYSTEM INTO A MODEL

Usually for sizing projects, each hardware server is represented in a model by a node with the number of the processing units equal to the number of CPUs. A three-tiered system hosting an enterprise application and its model are shown in Fig. 8.2. All application users are symbolized by the node "Users," and each server is mapped by a dedicated node. The connections among nodes indicate where a transaction can be processed after being served in a particular node. The "Web," "Application," and "Database" nodes have to be associated with particular hardware models (for example, all hardware servers are based on the Sun Fire X2270). The association is very important if the sizing project includes the evaluation of what-if scenarios for changing hardware platforms; it will let us use the relative system performance indicators provided by the benchmarks to compare application performance on different servers.

After the input data have been collected and the model has been built, we can solve it using the software packages discussed in Chapter 2.

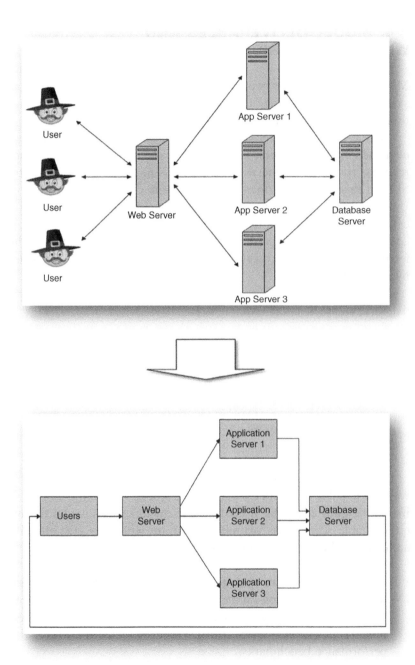

Figure 8.2. Model of a three-tiered system.

8.4. MODEL DELIVERABLES AND WHAT-IF SCENARIOS

Model solving produces two metrics critical for making decisions about system sizing: (1) average transaction response time for each transaction, and (2) utilization of each hardware server.

While considering the acceptability of architecture that has been evaluated by models, first we have to make certain that transaction response times are in line with the business requirements stated in the SLA. If that is the case, then next we have to check server utilization: Underutilization of the servers indicates that either they have excessive capacity or that there are too many of them; on both occasions system cost is unjustified. Sizing estimates have to recommend hardware architecture with the lowest cost that delivers the transaction times expected by a business.

Each modeling estimate is generated for a specified set of input data that includes:

- Workload
- Profile of each transaction
- Hardware architecture (number of servers, number of CPUs on each server, server types)
- Distribution (hosting) of an application's components among servers

Changing any of the above represents new what-if scenarios, and we have to solve the model to get a new estimate. The number of what-ifs can be quite high, but it is always smart to solve a model for any questionable scenario as we might come up with very cost-effective architecture. Let's discuss the most common what-if scenarios.

Changing hardware system. If an IT department has the option to host an application on the servers from different vendors or on servers from the same vendor but with different specifications, a model can generate sizing estimates for each scenario using relative performance benchmarks.

Cross-platform analysis. Many enterprise applications are platform independent; that means they can be hosted on diverse OSs

(Windows, AIX, HP-UX, LUNIX, etc.). The models can provide comparative data using benchmarks on relative performance of hardware systems with different OSs.

Workload variations. Each characteristic of a workload can fluctuate. The most obvious workload variation is the number of users. A business is not always ready to specify the number of application users, and it is looking for architectural proposals for different numbers of users. Two other variables are the number of users for a particular transaction as well as the transaction pacing rate. Workload definitely changes when the mix of transactions fluctuates; analyzing different mixes helps to identify system architecture with a minimal cost.

Remote users and network impact can be taken into account by analyzing various user distributions among remote offices as well as various network speeds.

Changing the number of CPUs. Increasing the number of CPUs on the same server provides additional capacity, and its effect can be evaluated by using relative performance benchmarks. CPU architectural specifics such as multi-core, hyper-threading, etc., also impact server capacity and can be assessed by the models.

Server farms. Adding servers changes model topology and requires definition of additional transaction profiles because new servers create new paths for transactions. For the model in Fig. 8.2, the profiles for transaction *Rule ABC* are presented in Table 8.8.

The table assumes that a load balancer distributes *Rule ABC* transactions among three "Application" servers; as a modeling input we have to specify three *Rule ABC* transactions processed by different "Application" servers.

Now let's add a "Web server"; a model with two "Web" servers is presented in Fig. 8.3.

The second "Web" server creates three new paths for transaction *Rule ABC*, and we have to define three new profiles (Table 8.9).

Adding the servers increases the number of paths a transaction can navigate across the system; each new path has to be associated with a new transaction profile; the number of paths can be significant for the

Table 8.8
Profiles of Transaction *Rule ABC*

Transaction Name	Time in Node "Web Server"	Time in Node "Application Server 1"	Time in Node "Application Server 2"	Time in Node "Application Server 3"	Time in Node "Database Server"	Expected Transaction Time
Rule ABC_1	1.0 sec	1.5 sec	N/A	N/A	2.5 sec	5.0 sec
Rule ABC_2	1.0 sec	N/A	1.5 sec	N/A	2.5 sec	5.0 sec
Rule ABC_3	1.0 sec	N/A	N/A	1.5 sec	2.5 sec	5.0 sec

Table 8.9
Profiles of Transaction *Rule ABC* for System With Two "Web" Servers

Transaction Name	Time in Node "Web Server 1"	Time in Node "Web Server 2"	Time in Node "Application Server 1"	Time in Node "Application Server 2"	Time in Node "Application Server 3"	Time in Node "Database Server"	Expected Transaction Time
Rule ABC_1	1.0 sec	N/A	1.5 sec	N/A	N/A	2.5 sec	5.0 sec
Rule ABC_2	1.0 sec	N/A	N/A	1.5 sec	N/A	2.5 sec	5.0 sec
Rule ABC_3	1.0 sec	N/A	N/A	N/A	1.5 sec	2.5 sec	5.0 sec
Rule ABC_4	N/A	1.0 sec	1.5 sec	N/A	N/A	2.5 sec	5.0 sec
Rule ABC_5	N/A	1.0 sec	N/A	1.5 sec	N/A	2.5 sec	5.0 sec
Rule ABC_6	N/A	1.0 sec	N/A	N/A	1.5 sec	2.5 sec	5.0 sec

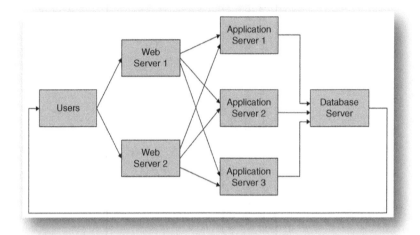

Figure 8.3. Model of three-tiered system with two "Web" servers and three "Application" servers.

Table 8.10
Distribution of Transaction *Rule ABC* Among a Farm's Servers

Transaction Name	Number of Users	Number of Transactions Per User Per Hour
Model With One "Web" and Three "Application" Servers (Fig. 8.2)		
Rule ABC_1	10	6
Rule ABC_2	10	6
Rule ABC_3	10	6
Model With Two "Web" and Three "Application" Servers (Fig. 8.3)		
Rule ABC_1	5	6
Rule ABC_2	5	6
Rule ABC_3	5	6
Rule ABC_4	5	6
Rule ABC_5	5	6
Rule ABC_6	5	6

large farms. The expected transaction time is the same as for transaction *Rule ABC* no matter in what farm's server it was processed.

Load distribution among clustered servers is carried out by a hardware or software load balancer. In both cases, the number of users per transaction specified by the workload has to be distributed among transactions navigating different paths and being served in different servers. An example of user redistribution is shown in Table 8.10 for a round-robin load balancing algorithm directing an equal number of transactions to each farm's server. A similar technique is applicable to various load balancing algorithms; for example, if the transactions generated by the users with computers on a particular network domain have to be directed to specified server, then we have to calculate the percentage of transactions generated from that domain and direct the same percentage to that specified server.

TAKE AWAY FROM THE CHAPTER

- *Enterprise applications are nonlinear systems featuring exponential-like explosions of transaction response times. Explosions are due to queues and queues are due to the random nature of events in complex systems as well as to the system's finite resources. Queuing models, among other factors, take into account waiting times in queues and provide more accurate sizing estimates than any empirical forecasts.*
- *Model-based application sizing includes:*
  - *Specification of a model's input data (workload, transaction profile, hardware platform, and expected transaction times)*
  - *Building the model*
  - *Solving the model*
  - *Analysis of modeling results*
  - *Analysis of different what-if scenarios in order to identify system architecture with the lowest cost and delivering the transaction times required by a business*

## CHAPTER 9

Modeling Different Application Configurations

In this chapter: performance implications of various enterprise application deployments and features (geographical distribution of users, remote terminal services, load balancing, and server farms; parallelization of single transaction processing, etc.).

9.1. GEOGRAPHICAL DISTRIBUTION OF USERS

Many corporations have offices all over the country or all over the world, which means application users are geographically distributed and access applications over network connections with various speeds. For that reason, users located in different offices will experience a fluctuation in transaction times. For example, for users working over a dial-in connection, accessing the application might be unacceptably slow; for the users accessing the application over a corporate network it might seem quite fast.

Figure 9.1 presents the model of an application with the users located in two places—New York and Nairobi, Kenya. Servers are

Solving Enterprise Applications Performance Puzzles: Queuing Models to the Rescue, First Edition. Leonid Grinshpan.
© 2012 Institute of Electrical and Electronics Engineers. Published 2012 by John Wiley & Sons, Inc.

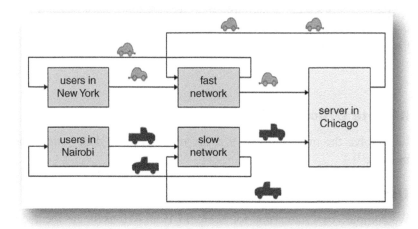

Figure 9.1. Model of an application with users in different locations.

deployed at a corporate data center in Chicago. New York users are connected over a fast corporate network; Nairobi's users are connected over a slow dial-in connection. To distinguish requests from two different user groups we introduce two car types—the sedans symbolize the requests from New York users and the trucks stand for the requests from Nairobi users.

Because of the difference in network speed, it is evident that the time of the same business transaction will be longer for Nairobi users than for New York users. The model in Fig. 9.1 takes into account the existence of two user groups connected to the servers over the networks with different speeds; for that reason, this model is capable of calculating transaction times for the user in New York as well as for the user in Nairobi.

A network delay impacts the **Rate of incoming requests** for each server: the longer the delay, the lower the **Rate of incoming requests.** If an equal number of users in New York and Nairobi are involved in the same business activity and requesting the same transactions, then request-trucks originating in Nairobi will hit the servers in Chicago with a lower intensity than request-sedans that originated in New York because of the slower network for the Nairobi users. Actually, a slow network offloads servers as it takes more time for requests to travel from users to servers.

A slow network brings down utilization of system servers because it takes longer for a user request to reach the server over a slow network; it also takes longer for system replies to reach users' computers.

Remote Office Models

Let's solve the model in Fig. 9.1; the model's input data is described in Table 9.1.

Users' Locations

We compare two scenarios: for Scenario 1, all 410 users are located in New York. For Scenario 2, only 210 users work from New York; the remaining 200 users access the application from Nairobi.

User think times and transaction profiles are presented in Table 9.2.

The model suggests (Chart 9.1) that there is a noticeable improvement in transaction time for New York users when users are distributed per Scenario 2. This improvement can be attributed to a decrease in server utilization due to the network delays for remote users.

Table 9.1

Input Data for "Remote Office" Model: Workload Characterization

	Average Number of Transactions Per User Per Hour	Number Of Users	
Transaction Name		*Scenario 1* (Local) 410 Users in New York	*Scenario 2 (Distributed)* 210 Users in New York and 200 Users In Nairobi
New York Users			
Sales Report	2	300	150
Income Statement	5	100	50
Profit and Loss Report	2	10	10
Nairobi Users			
Sales Report	2	0	150
Income Statement	5	0	50

Table 9.2

Input Data for "Remote Office" Model: User Think Time and Transaction Profile

Transaction Name	User Location	User Think Time (Seconds)		Transaction Profile (Seconds)		
		Node "Users In Nairobi"	Node "Users in New York"	Node "Fast Network"	Node "Slow Network"	Node "Server in Chicago"
Sales report	New York	—	1,800	5	—	20
Sales report	Nairobi	720	—		15	25
Income statement	New York	—	720	5	—	30
Income statement	Nairobi	720	—	—	15	35
Profit and loss report	New York	—	1,800	5 Sec	—	35

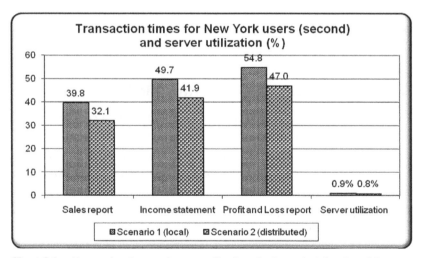

Chart 9.1.   Transaction times and server utilizations for Scenario 1 (local) and Scenario 2 (distributed).

Network Latency

Let's find out how network latency affects application performance for local users. We solve the model for 15 sec and 30 sec times in node "slow network"; that means we are comparing two networks with different latencies. Per Chart 9.2 there is a transaction time

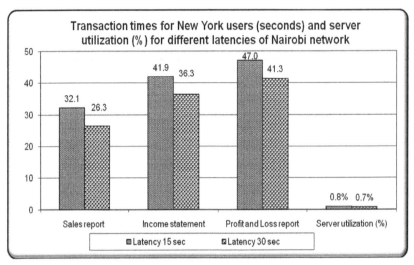

Chart 9.2. Transaction times and server utilizations for different network latencies.

improvement for the New York office as the latency of the slow network increases.

Take Away from Remote Office Models

- *Geographical distribution of users brings server utilizations down because of network delays for remote users*
- *Moving users from local to remote offices results in transaction time improvement for the local users connected to the servers over fast networks*
- *Higher network latency for remote offices enables faster transactions for local users*

9.2. ACCOUNTING FOR THE TIME ON END-USER COMPUTERS

In the endless pursuit for perfect application architecture, an application's components located on the end-user's computer experience fluctuations in functionality. At one end of that spectrum, there is the

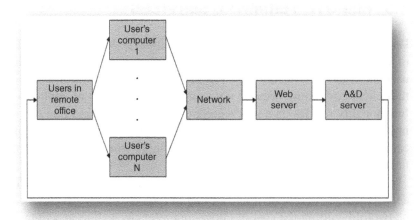

Figure 9.2.   System with end-user computer.

so-called thin client capable of only rendering text and pictures; at the opposite end is a client-server environment where a server is a database, and the client is responsible for all business logic as well as data presentation.

Between these two poles lies a wide array of client implementations. Web 2.0 technologies such as Ajax, Java script, Dojo, Flex, jQuery, and similar ones are capable of executing significant processing on a client computer and contributing to the total transaction time. Enterprise applications with a spreadsheet client (like Excel) often exploit to the full extent its rich functionality, making client-side processing significantly longer than server-side processing. When and if there is a need to take into account client-side processing time, we can build a model with additional nodes that represent the end-user computer (Fig. 9.2).

The model includes as many "User's computer" nodes for as many users as the system has. Each such node serves only one transaction at a time and for that it has only one processing unit and never has any requests in a queue. The processing time in each "User's computer" node depends on the computer specifications it represents; this allows us to estimate transaction response times for users working from a variety of front end computers.

9.3. REMOTE TERMINAL SERVICES

Remote terminal services (RTS) (the terminology varies from vendor to vendor) deliver to the end user only an image of the application's user interface. The technology represents the ultimate incarnation of thin-client computing because not even the smallest part of application functionality resides on a user's computer. A user's workstation can be implemented as a low-end terminal capable of only rendering an application's visual interface on its monitor. An input from the user is transferred to a system where it is processed.

Enterprise application architects in some cases consider RTS deployment for corporate users located in remote offices. The goal can be twofold: cutting the cost of client computers as well as speeding up transactions over slow network connections. The latter can be evaluated using models for the configurations with and without RTS.

All models analyzed so far in this book have represented application deployments without RTS; they included nodes modeling the user as well as the network that connects remote users and application. In deployments without RTS, a full volume of data generated by the application in response to a user's request is transferred over a network. If that volume is large and the network is slow, then substantial time can be added to each transaction, and remote users will consider the system as unacceptably slow.

To speed up transactions, a connection of remote users over RTS can be helpful, and its effect can be evaluated using the model in Fig. 9.3.

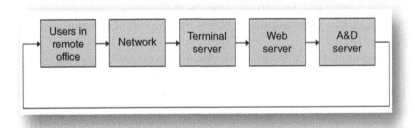

Figure 9.3. System with RTS.

The model of a system with RTS does not feature "User's computer" nodes as an RTS goal is to minimize time on the client side. A system with RTS has an additional "Terminal server" in charge of maintaining and managing remote terminal sessions. On the one hand, by including the "Terminal server" we have introduced an additional component in the transaction profile, as transactions have to be processed by the "Terminal server." On the other hand, a system with RTS delivers a smaller volume of data to a user and expectations are that the transaction will spend less time in a network. Our models can predict if a decrease in network time is significant enough to compensate for additional processing time in the "Terminal server." The "Terminal server" also has to have an adequate capacity to execute concurrently multiple client-side processing otherwise it might become a bottleneck; for that reason, the suitability of RTS for the applications with rich functionality on a client computer (thick-client) can be limited.

Remote terminal services speed up transaction times for remote users only if a decrease in network time is significant enough to compensate for the additional time a transaction is processed by the "Terminal server." That is often not a case for the applications with rich functionality on a client computer. The "Terminal server" can create a bottleneck if its capacity is not sufficient for concurrent processing of data for multiple users.

9.4. CROSS-PLATFORM MODELING

Among the many questions a performance analyst faces while planning system capacity, there is one that stands out: What would system performance be if server A running OS X is replaced with a server B running OS Y? Such a what-if scenario requires an evaluation of hardware models that host different OSs. The benchmark SPEC CPU2006 helps to answer to that question.

As we know, SPEC CPU2006 contains two benchmarks: CINT2006, which executes predominantly integer instructions, and CFP2006, which executes predominantly floating-point instructions. Both benchmarks have been conducted on servers with different operating systems; some of the systems are:

- Red Hat Enterprise Linux Server release 5.3, Kernel 2.6.18-128. el5
- SUSE Linux Enterprise Server 10 (x86_64) SP2, Kernel 2.6.16.60-0.21-smp
- Solaris 10 11/06
- Windows Vista32 Business
- Windows Vista Ultimate w/ SP1 (64-bit)
- AIX 5L V5.3
- Windows Server 2003 Enterprise Edition (32 bits), Service Pack1
- HPUX11i-TCOE B.11.23.0609
- SUSE Linux Enterprise Server 10 64-bit kernel

Here is a benchmark's information for the same Sun server running OpenSolaris and Linux OSs:

System	Sun Fire X2270 (Intel Xeon X5570 2.93 GHz)	Sun Fire X2270 (Intel Xeon X5570 2.93 GHz)
Benchmark	CINT2006	CINT2006
Baseline	**29.6**	**30.5**
# Core	8	8
# Chips	2	2
# Core Per Chip	4	4
# Threads	2	2
Processor	Intel Xeon X5570	Intel Xeon X5570
Memory	24 GB (6 × 4 GB DDR3-1333	24 GB (6 × 4 GB DDR3-1333
Operating system	OpenSolaris 2008.11	SuSe Linux Enterprise Server 10 (x86_64), SP2, Kernel 2.6.16.60-0.21-smp

It can be seen that the relative performance for CINT2006 benchmark slightly differs for the two OSs (see the row "Baseline"). Benchmark CFP2006 points at a larger difference between the same systems:

System	Sun Fire X2270 (Intel Xeon X5570 2.93 GHz)	Sun Fire X2270 (Intel Xeon X5570 2.93 GHz)
Benchmark	CFP2006	CFP2006
Operating system	OpenSolaris 2008.11	SuSe Linux Enterprise Server 10 (x86_64), SP2, Kernel 2.6.16.60-0.21-smp
Baseline	**43.6**	**32.8**

Benchmark SPEC CPU2006 has data on performance of the same servers under the Linux and Windows OSs. This is often a topic of heated discussions between proponents of each OS. Below are the results for server Dell Precision T7500 (Intel Xeon W5590, 3.33 GHz):

System	Dell Precision T7500 (Intel Xeon W5590, 3.33 GHz)	Dell Precision T7500 (Intel Xeon W5590, 3.33 GHz)
Operating System	Red Hat Enterprise Linux Client release 5.3, Kernel 2.6.18-128.el5 on an x86_64	Windows Vista Business SP1 (64-bit)
Baseline (Benchmark CINT2006)	**33.8**	**33.1**
Baseline (Benchmark CFP2006)	**39.6**	**37.4**

9.5. LOAD BALANCING AND SERVER FARMS

The scalability of enterprise applications is based on their ability to use multiple servers on different tiers to keep transaction times acceptable under increasing workloads. A scalable application is capable of distributing a workload among a number of servers; such functionality is reflected in queuing models by multiple nodes representing a server farm (Fig. 9.4 pictures a model with three "Web" and two "A&D" servers).

To describe a workload distribution in a model of an application deployed on a server farm, we can use a matrix with the probabilities of transitions from node to node. Table 9.3 illustrates a transaction's

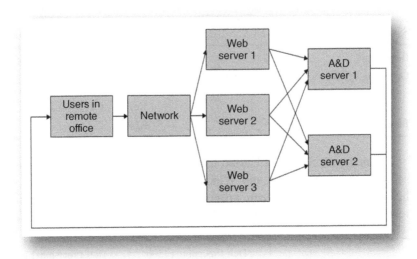

Figure 9.4. Modeling server farms.

Table 9.3
Transition Matrix for Even Workload Distribution Among Servers

	Users	Network	"Web Server 1"	"Web Server 2"	"Web Server 3"	"A&D Server 1"	"A&D Server 2"
Users	0	1	0	0	0	0	0
Network	0	0	0.333	0.333	0.333	0	0
"Web server 1"	0	0	0	0	0	0.5	0.5
"Web server 2"	0	0	0	0	0	0.5	0.5
"Web server 3"	0	0	0	0	0	0.5	0.5
"A&D server 1"	1	0	0	0	0	0	0
"A&D server 2"	1	0	0	0	0	0	0

transitions among system nodes when the load balancers between the "Web" servers and between the "A&D" servers are using even workload distributions.

A transaction initiated by a user with a probability of 1 is transferred over the network; after that a "Web" tier load balancer with a probability of 0.333 directs the request to one of three "Web" servers. From each "Web" server a request with a probability of 0.5 is directed to one of two "A&D" servers. Finally, the request processed by an "A&D" server request returns to the user.

A transition matrix can depict any itineraries among the nodes; it also models load balancing algorithms by assigning the values to transaction probabilities. If the load balancing algorithm is based on node utilizations, then transaction probability is a function of the node's utilization and should be calculated during model solving.

> The transition matrix specifies transaction itineraries as well as load balancing algorithms.

9.6. TRANSACTION PARALLEL PROCESSING MODELS

In order to speed up transaction processing, some enterprise applications are capable of organizing parallel processing of the same transaction using multithreaded software architecture. We analyze two approaches to transaction parallelization—concurrent processing of a single transaction by a few servers, and concurrent processing of a single transaction by either a few CPUs or a CPU and an I/O subsystem of the same server.

Concurrent Transaction Processing by a Few Servers

Transaction parallelization is implemented by breaking down the transaction into a few tasks that can be executed concurrently on different hardware servers. To demonstrate how a model reflects such functionality, we refer to the one pictured in Fig. 9.5; it has four nodes representing "Users," "Web server," "Application server," and OLAP

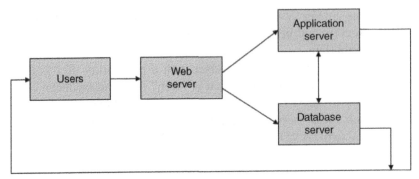

Figure 9.5. Model of application enabling transaction parallel processing in different servers.

Table 9.4
Workload Characterization, Non-Parallelized Transactions

Transaction Name	Number of Users	Number of Transactions Per User Per Hour
Report ABC	20, 40, 60 . . . 180	10
Business rule XYZ	20, 40, 60 . . . 180	10

Table 9.5
Transaction Profiles, Non-Parallelized Transactions (in seconds)

Transaction Name	"Web Server"	"Application Server"	"Database Server"
Report ABC	1	1	3
Business rule XYZ	2	3	15

"Database server." The "Web" and "Application" server nodes have four processing units each; the "Database server" has eight processing units.

Workload is characterized by Table 9.4 and includes two transactions: *Report ABC* and *Business rule XYZ*. Transaction profiles are specified in Table 9.5.

We assume that transaction *Report ABC* cannot be broken down by tasks and has to be processed only on a single thread. Conversely, the transaction *Business rule XYZ* is suitable for parallel processing: while the data for the business rule is calculated by the OLAP "Database server," the "Application server" is also working preparing forms and charts to be delivered to the user. We can imagine that transaction *Business rule XYZ* is divided by two "derivative" transactions right after leaving "Web server"; one goes into "Application server" and the second one visits "Database" server." For a parallelized transaction, the total response time will include only the longest processing time it spent either on the "Application" or "Database" servers.

To analyze the parallelization effect we break down transaction *Business rule XYZ* by three "derivative" ones with profiles described in Table 9.6.

After transaction breakdown, a new workload is characterized as seen in Table 9.7.

Table 9.6

Transaction Profiles, Parallelized Transaction *Business Rule XYZ* (in seconds)

Transaction Name	"Web Server"	"Application Server"	"Database Server"
Report ABC	1	1	3
Business rule XYZ_W	2	0	0
Business rule XYZ_A	0	3	0
Business rule XYZ_D	0	0	15

Table 9.7

Workload Characterization, Parallelized Transaction *Business Rule XYZ*

Transaction Name	Number of Users	Number of Transactions Per User Per Hour
Report ABC	20, 40, 60 . . . 180	10
Business rule XYZ_W	20, 40, 60 . . . 180	10
Business rule XYZ_A	20, 40, 60 . . . 180	10
Business rule XYZ_D	20, 40, 60 . . . 180	10

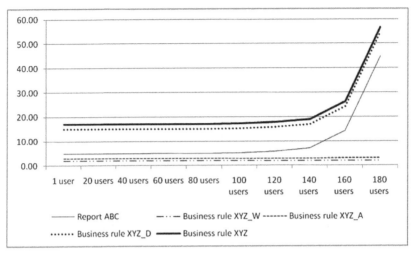

Chart 9.3. Transaction times (in seconds) for transaction profiles from Table 9.7.

The novelty of that workload is only in the updated transaction list; its demand for system service is unchanged. The total time of transaction *Business rule XYZ* has to be calculated per the formula:

Business rule XYZ =

$$\text{Business rule XYZ\_W} + \max \begin{cases} \text{Business rule XYZ\_A} \\ \text{Business rule XYZ\_D} \end{cases}$$

Transaction times as evaluated by the model are shown in Chart 9.3. The total time of *Business rule XYZ* is composed of the times in the "Web" and "Database" servers, as the latter is longer than time spent in "Application server."

The profile of transaction *Report ABC* has a remarkable impact on the time of transaction *Business rule XYZ*. If we change the service demand of *Report ABC* for the "Application server" from 1 sec to 20 sec, then for the number of users from 1 to 60, the time of *Business rule XYZ* is composed of the times in the "Web" and "Database" servers; above 60 users it includes the time spent in the "Web" and "Application" servers (Chart 9.4).

An explanation can be found in Chart 9.5 that shows the utilization of all system servers. When the number of users exceeds 60, "Application server" utilization grows beyond 90%; such a high level slows down processing of *Business rule XYZ_A* transactions.

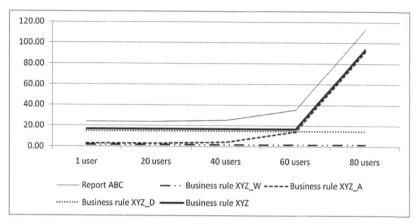

Chart 9.4. Transaction times (in seconds) for the updated *Report ABC* profile.

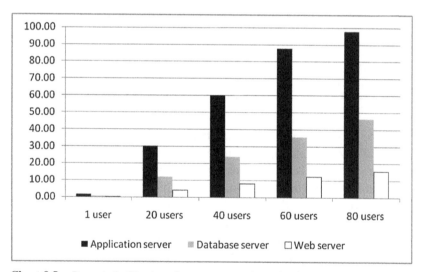

Chart 9.5. Percent of utilization of system servers for updated *Report ABC* profile.

Concurrent Transaction Processing by the Same Server

Parallelization of transaction processing within the same server is achieved by two ways: (1) concurrent processing by a number of CPUs; (2) concurrent processing by a CPU and an I/O system.

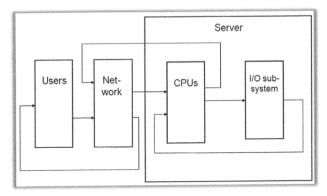

Figure 9.6. Model to study the effect of parallelization on transaction processing within a single server.

Table 9.8
Transaction Profiles, Non-Parallelized Transactions (in seconds)

Transaction Name	Network	I/O Subsystem	CPUs
Report ABC	0.5	1.5	3
Business rule XYZ	0.5	4.5	15

The model in Fig. 9.6 is suitable to study the effects of this kind of parallelization on application performance.

The model has four nodes: two nodes without queues represent users and the network, and two nodes with queues correspond to hardware server CPUs and an I/O subsystem. We assume that node "CPUs" has eight processing units; node "I/O subsystem" with four processing units characterizes four disks. For non-parallelized transactions, the workload is described in Table 9.4 and the transaction profiles in Table 9.8.

Let's suppose transaction *Business rule XYZ* can be executed in node "CPUs" on two threads concurrently; in such a case its service demand for the "CPUs" node is two times lower and equal to 7.5 sec, but the transaction will demand two CPUs. Running the transaction *Business rule XYZ* on two threads accounts for breaking it down by two "derivative" transactions: *Business rule XYZ_1* and *Business rule XYZ_2*. Workload characterization and transaction profiles are described in Tables 9.9 and 9.10.

Table 9.9

Workload Characterization : Transactions *Business rule XYZ*
Executed on Two Threads

Transaction Name	Number of Users	Number of Transactions Per User Per Hour
Report ABC	20, 40, 60 . . . 180	10
Business rule XYZ_1	20, 40, 60 . . . 180	10
Business rule XYZ_2	20, 40, 60 . . . 180	10

Table 9.10

Transaction Profiles (in seconds): Transactions *Business rule XYZ* Executed on Two Threads

Transaction Name	Network	I/O Subsystem	CPUs
Report ABC	0.5	1.5	3
Business rule XYZ_1	0.5	4.5	7.5
Business rule XYZ_2	0.5	4.5	7.5

Chart 9.6 compares response times for non-parallelized and parallelized transaction *Business rule XYZ.*

The parallelized transaction features better a response time until the number of users is under 120; after that its time gets much longer than for the non-parallelized transaction. Chart 9.7 identifies what causes the "hockey stick" effect.

The "I/O subsystem" node is loaded noticeably higher when the transaction is processed on two threads. In this instance, service demand for the "CPUs" node is two times lower, but the rate of transactions coming into the "I/O subsystem" node is higher. For 120 users, "I/O subsystem" utilization reached 85%, slowing down I/O operations and impacting transaction response time. That modeling result is to some extent counterintuitive—we would expect an increase in the "CPUs" node utilization by parallelized transactions but apparently it is compensated for by a shorter demand time. "CPUs" node utilizations are practically equal for parallelized and non-parallelized scenarios as long as the number of users does not exceed 120 (Chart 9.8).

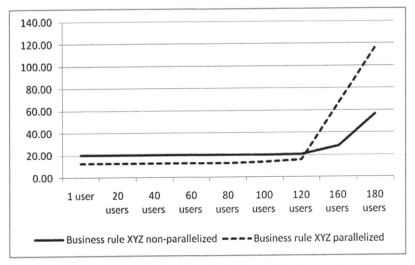

Chart 9.6. Response times for non-parallelized and parallelized transaction *Business rule XYZ.*

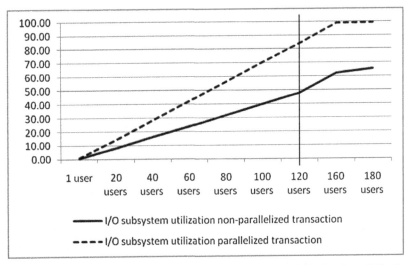

Chart 9.7. I/O subsystem utilization (percentage) for non-parallelized and parallelized transaction *Business rule XYZ.*

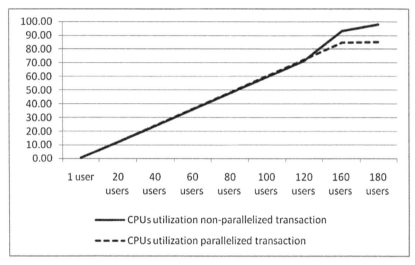

Chart 9.8. "CPUs" node utilization (percentage) for non-parallelized and parallelized transaction *Business rule XYZ*.

Take Away from Transaction Parallel Processing Models

- *For modeling different transaction parallelization techniques we can employ the same closed queuing networks with a constant number of requests that we have used in previous chapters. Accounting for transaction parallelization is implemented by breaking down a single multithreaded transaction into a number of "derivative" transactions equal to the number of threads.*

- *Workload characterization, as well as transaction profiles, have to be defined for "derivative" transactions. The number of users and transaction rate for each "derivative" transaction are the same as for the original multithreaded transaction.*

- *The multithreading impact on transaction response time and utilization of hardware resources can be counterintuitive; queuing models provide numeric estimates of such impacts and determine the cause/effect relationship of parallelization.*

TAKE AWAY FROM THE CHAPTER

- *The speed and latency of the network's connection from a corporation's remote offices to data centers influence transaction times for all application users; they also weigh on server utilizations.*

- *As industry moves toward a thick-client paradigm, processing time on end-user computers can be quite noticeable, and it has to be added to transaction response time.*

- *Remote terminal services speed up transaction time for remote users only if a decrease in network time is significant enough to compensate for the additional time a transaction is processed by a specialized terminal server. The terminal server can create a bottleneck if its capacity is not sufficient for concurrent processing of data for multiple users.*

- *Frequently asked question about performance of the same application on platforms with different OSs can be answered by solving the same model for a number of input data provided by benchmarks for different OSs.*

- *A transition matrix depicts complicated transaction itineraries as well as load balancing algorithms when an application is deployed on server farms with load balancers.*

- *The discussed approach to modeling multithreaded transactions helps obtain numeric estimates of the impact of transaction parallelization on system performance.*

Glossary

Application performance management (APM): Process and use of related IT tools to detect, diagnose, remedy, and report an application's performance to ensure that it meets or exceeds end-users' and businesses' expectations. Application performance relates to how fast transactions are completed on behalf of, or the information is delivered to the end-user by the application via a particular network, application, and/or Web services infrastructure (source: http://en.wikipedia.org/wiki/Application_performance_management).

Application scalability: The application's ability to maintain an acceptable transaction time (as determined by users) under an increasing workload by utilizing additional or faster hardware components (servers, CPUs, etc.).

Application tuning: A course of action aimed at the identification and fixing of bottlenecks in deployed applications.

Application workload: A flow of transactions initiated by users forcing an application to do some amount of work in order to generate replies; it is specified by workload characterization.

Benchmark SPEC CPU2006: CPU2006 is SPEC's next-generation, industry-standardized, CPU-intensive benchmark suite, stressing a system's processor, memory subsystem, and compiler. SPEC designed CPU2006 to provide a comparative measure of compute-intensive performance across the widest practical range of hardware using workloads developed from real user applications (source: http://www.spec.org/cpu2006/).

Capacity planning (also known as application sizing): Process of obtaining estimates of hardware architecture capable of providing the requested service quality for the anticipated workload.

Closed queuing network: Queuing network with a constant number of transactions.

Solving Enterprise Applications Performance Puzzles: Queuing Models to the Rescue, First Edition. Leonid Grinshpan.
© 2012 Institute of Electrical and Electronics Engineers. Published 2012 by John Wiley & Sons, Inc.

Client-server architecture: Computer system design where user (client) works with a client program; through this program the user demands a service from a server program by sending a request over a corporate network. The client program resides on the user's computer; the server program is hosted on a server.

Enterprise application: Computer system supporting implementation of critical business functions of corporations; it includes business-oriented software, hardware infrastructure that hosts it, as well as operating systems.

Interactive application: Application that prevents the user from submitting the next transaction request before a reply to the previous one was received. The majority of enterprise applications are interactive because they have to support execution of business taskflows broken down by a number of steps where each subsequent step depends on the results of the previous ones.

Little's Law: A formula $L = \lambda*W$, where L is the average number of requests in a node and W is the average time a single request spends in a node (in its queue and processing unit). The significance of the formula is in its applicability to any node inside the network, to any subset of nodes, as well as to the whole queuing network. A key derivative from Little's Law is a formula defining the average time T a request spends in a node's queue and processing unit: $T = 1/(\mu - \lambda)$.

Load generator: Software package that generates a workload by simulating the activity of an application's users.

Mean value analysis: A technique to solve closed queuing networks based on a computational algorithm.

Model calibration: A process ensuring that a model generates output data (transaction response times, server utilizations, etc.) close to the ones observed in a real production system.

Model input data: Consists of workload characterization and transaction profiles.

Model solver: As defined in http://en.wikipedia.org/wiki/Solver: "A solver is a generic term indicating a piece of mathematical software, possibly in the form of a stand-alone computer program or as a software library that 'solves' a mathematical problem. A solver takes problem descriptions in some sort of generic form and calculates their solution." A model solver is all of above with respect to queuing models.

Model topology: A graph consisting of the nodes and the connections among them; users and hardware components are represented by the nodes; connections between nodes depict transaction paths in an application.

Multithreaded application: An application designed in a way that it is capable of enacting two kinds of parallelization by spawning software threads:

- Serving concurrently multiple transactions initiated by different users
- Breaking down a single transaction by multiple independent tasks and executing them either in a few CPUs or in a CPU and an I/O subsystem

Multithreaded architecture is pervasive in enterprise applications because it enables an application to use available hardware resources to the fullest extent.

Node: A component of the queuing model that in general includes the processing unit and queue.

Node's processing rate: A number of requests a node can process per a particular time interval.

Number of active application users: Quantity of users logged into an application and working with it.

Number of concurrent application users: Quantity of users waiting for replies from the system to their requests. Only concurrent users consume system resources.

Number of total application users: Equal to the number of users having access to an application (they have user names, passwords, and are provisioned accordingly).

OLAP: Abbreviation for online analytical processing. The technology capable of satisfying complex analytical and ad-hoc queries; it is based on multidimensional databases.

Open queuing network: Queuing network with a changing number of transactions.

Process (in computing context): An instance of a computer program that is currently active on a hardware server processing transactions.

Processing unit: A component of a node that serves requests.

Queuing network node: A component of a queuing network that consists of the queue and processing units. Incoming requests are served in the processing unit immediately if there are no waiting requests in the queue; otherwise, they are placed in the queue and wait until the processing unit becomes available.

Rate of node's incoming requests: A number of requests coming into a node per a particular time interval.

Rate of user requests: A number of requests submitted by one user for a given time interval, usually one hour.

Remote terminal services (RTS): Technology that delivers to the end-user's computer only an image of an application's user interface; it represents the ultimate incarnation of thin-client computing because not even the smallest part of the application functionality resides on a user's computer.

Service demand: Time interval a transaction spends in a processing unit receiving service.

Service level agreement (SLA): A document specifying services and their quality that a business expects to be provided by an application to its users. Contains important information for application performance tuning and sizing requirements such as transaction response times and estimates of the workload an application has to support.

Simulation: A technique to solve queuing networks based on computer simulation of requests waiting in queues and served in processing units.

Software instrumentation: The ability of a computer program to collect and report data on its performance. The performance of an instrumented application can be analyzed and managed using a management tool.

Storage area network (SAN): Storage appliances designed in a way that they appear to the hardware server as local disks; because of high data transfer speed, they are a well-accepted component of enterprise application infrastructure. Unlike SAN, network-attached storage appliances more often serve as shared file storage systems.

Transaction: An amount of work performed by an application to satisfy a user's request. Various publications on queuing models do not distinguish between terms "request" and "transaction," assuming they mean the same; that is also the case for this book.

Transaction profile: A set of time intervals (service demands) a transaction has spent in all processing units it has visited while served by an application.

Transaction rate: Number of transaction requests submitted by one user at particular time interval, usually during one hour. Correlated with user think time: **transaction rate = 3600 seconds/user think time**.

Transaction (response) time: Time to process a transaction by an application.

Thread: An object created by a program to execute a single task. A program spawns multiple threads to process a number of tasks concurrently. Technically, a thread is a sequence of an application's code statements that are executed one by one by a CPU. A single-threaded application can use only one CPU; a multithreaded application is able to create a few concurrent code flows and to load a few CPUs at the same time as well as an I/O system.

User request: A demand for service sent by a user to an application. Various publications on queuing models do not distinguish between terms "request" and "transaction," assuming they mean the same.

User think time: Period when a user analyzes a reply from an application for a particular transaction and prepares a new transaction. Correlated with transaction rate: **user think time = 3,600 seconds/transaction rate**.

Workload characterization: Specification of workload that includes three components: (1) list of business transactions; (2) for each transaction the number of its executions at a particular time interval (usually during one hour) per request from one user. That number is called transaction rate; (3) for each transaction a number of users requesting it.

References

[1.1] Robert Orfali, Dan Harkley, and Jeri Edvards. 1999. *Client/Server Survival Guide*, 3rd ed. New York: Wiley.

[1.2] Connie U. Smith. 1990. *Performance Engineering of Software Systems.* Reading, MA: Addison-Wesley Publishing Company.

[1.3] Neil J. Gunther. 2010. *Guerrilla Capacity Planning: A Tactical Approach to Planning for Highly Scalable Applications and Services.* New York: Springer.

[1.4] Daniel A. Menasce, Lawrence W. Dowdy, and Virgilio A.F. Almeida. 2004. *Performance by Design: Computer Capacity Planning By Example.* Upper Saddle River, NJ: Prentice Hall.

[2.1] Edward D. Lazowska, John Zahorjan, G. Scott Graham, and Kenneth C. Sevcik. 1984. *Quantitative System Performance. Computer System Analysis Using Queueing Network Models.* Englewood Cliffs, NJ: Prentice-Hall, Inc.

[2.2] Karl Sigman. 2009. "Notes on Little's Law." Posted online at http://www.columbia.edu/~ks20/stochastic-I/stochastic-I-LL.pdf.

[2.3] Jeffrey P. Buzen. 1973. "Computational Algorithms for Closed Queueing Networks With Exponential Servers." *CACM* 16(9): 527–531.

[2.4] M. Reiser and S.S. Lavenberg. 1980. "Mean Value Analysis of Closed Multi-Chain Queuing Networks." *JACM* 27: 313–322.

[2.5] Reuven Y. Rubinstein and Dirk P. Kroese. 2007. *Simulation and the Monte Carlo Method*, 2nd ed. Hoboken, NJ: Wiley.

[2.6] Humayun Akhtar, Ph.D. AT&T Laboratories. 1997. "An Overview of Some Network Modeling, Simulation & Performance Analysis Tools." *Proceedings of the Second IEEE Symposium on Computers and Communications*, Alexandria, Egypt, pp. 344–348. Posted online at http://bnnsolutions.com/OverOfSome_1.pdf.

[2.7] M. Bertoli, G. Casale, and G. Serazzi. 2007. "An Overview of the JMT Queueing Network Simulator." Technical Report TR 2007.2, Politecnico di Milano—DEI. Posted online at http://jmt.sourceforge.net/Documentation.html.

[2.8] Mark Friedman and Odysseas Pentakalos. 2002. *Windows 2000 Performance Guide.* Sebastopol, CA: O'Reilly Media.

Solving Enterprise Applications Performance Puzzles: Queuing Models to the Rescue, First Edition. Leonid Grinshpan.
© 2012 Institute of Electrical and Electronics Engineers. Published 2012 by John Wiley & Sons, Inc.

[2.9] Adrian Cockcroft and Richard Pettit. 1998. *Sun Performance and Tuning: Java and the Internet*. Englewood Cliffs, NJ: Prentice Hall.

[3.1] Definition of workload, http://en.wikipedia.org/wiki/Workload#Workload_Theory_and_Workload_Modelling.

[3.2] LoadRunner by Hewlett Packard (https://h10078.www1.hp.com/cda/hpms/display/main/hpms_content.jsp?zn=bto&cp=1-11-15-17∧8_4000_100__).

[3.3] Rational Performance Tester by IBM (http://www-01.ibm.com/software/awdtools/tester/performance/).

[3.4] Silk Performer by Borland (http://www.borland.com/us/products/silk/silkperformer/).

[3.5] Oracle Application Testing Suite by Oracle (http://www.oracle.com/technetwork/oem/app-test/index.html).

[3.6] Alec Sharp and Patrick McDermott. 2008. *Workflow Modeling: Tools for Process Improvement and Application Development*. Boston: Artech House.

[3.7] Michael Havey. 2005. *Essential Business Process Modeling*. Sebastopol, CA: O'Reilly Media.

[3.8] Definition of a process in computing context, http://en.wikipedia.org/wiki/Process_(computing).

[3.9] Brian Clifton. 2010. *Advanced Web Metrics with Google Analytics*, 2nd ed. Sybex.

[3.10] Avinash Kaushik. 2009. *Web Analytics 2.0: The Art of Online Accountability and Science of Customer Centricity*. Sybex.

[3.11] Oracle Real User Experience Insight (http://www.oracle.com/technetwork/oem/uxinsight/index.html).

[3.12] "Correlsense and Metron: Transaction-Based Capacity Planning for Greater IT Reliability™: A White Paper." Posted online at http://www.correlsense.com/sites/default/files/Correlsense-Metron-Transaction-Based-Capacity-Planning_White%20Paper.2.pdf.

[3.13] CoreFirst by OpTier (http://www.optier.com/corefirst_overview.aspx).

[3.14] *Proceedings of the IEEE 2005—2010 International Symposiums on Workload Characterization*, IISWC-2011, November 6–8, 2011, Austin, TX (http://www.iiswc.org). This symposium is dedicated to the understanding and characterization of the workloads that run on all types of computing systems.

[3.15] J. Buzen and B. Zibitsker. 2006. "Workload Characterization for Parallel Processing Environments." Presentation at CMG 2005, Orlando, FL; and UKCMG 2006, Warwick, England. CMG Magazine.

[3.16] Priya Nagpurkar, William Horn, U. Gopalakrishnan, Niteesh Dubey, Joefon Jann, and Pratap Pattnaik. 2008. "Workload Characterization of Selected JEE-Based Web 2.0 Applications." IBM T.J. Watson Research Center (Posted online at http://domino.research.ibm.com/comm/research_people.nsf/pages/nagpurkar.pubs.html/$FILE/web20-iiswc08.pdf).

[3.17] Yefim Shuf and Ian M. Steiner. 2007. "Characterizing a Complex J2EE Workload: A Comprehensive Analysis and Opportunities for Optimizations."

International Symposium on Analysis of Systems and Software (ISPASS), San Jose, CA, pp. 44–53.

[3.18] Michael A. Salsburg. "Workload Characterization and Modeling for High Performance Computing." Posted online at http://www.cmg.org/measureit/ issues/mit09/m_9_3.html, November 1, 2003.

[4.1] David A. Patterson and John L. Hennessy. 2008. *Computer Organization and Design: The Hardware/Software Interface*, 4th ed. Burlington, MA: Morgan Kaufmann.

[4.2] Stanislav Garmatyuk. "How CPU Features Affect CPU Performance, Part 4." Posted online at http://ixbtlabs.com/articles3/cpu/archspeed-2009-4-p1.html, October 15, 2009.

[5.1] Andrew S. Tanenbaum. 2008. *Modern Operating Systems*. Upper Saddle River, NJ: Prentice Hall.

[5.2] Abraham Silberschatz, Peter B. Galvin, and Greg Gagne. 2008. *Operating System Concepts*, 8th ed. Hoboken, NJ: Wiley.

[5.3] Thomas Rauber and Gudula Rünger. 2010. *Parallel Programming: For Multicore and Cluster Systems*. New York: Springer.

[5.4] Rudy Chukran. 2008. *Accelerating AIX: Performance Tuning for Programmers and Systems Administrators*, Reading, MA: Addison-Wesley Professional.

[5.5] Sandra K. Johnson, Gerrit Huizenga, and Badari Pulavarty. 2005. *Performance Tuning for Linux(R) Servers*. Indianapolis, IN: IBM Press.

[5.6] Robert F. Sauers, Chris P. Ruemmler, and Peter S. Weygant. 2004. *HP-UX 11i Tuning and Performance*. Upper Saddle River, NJ: Prentice Hall.

[6.1] Maurice Herlihy and Nir Shavit. 2008. *The Art of Multiprocessor Programming*. Boston: Morgan Kaufmann.

[6.2] Joe Duffy. 2008. *Concurrent Programming on Windows*. Reading, MA: Addison-Wesley Professional.

[6.3] Clay Breshears. 2009. *The Art of Concurrency: A Thread Monkey's Guide to Writing Parallel Applications*. Sebastopol, CA: O'Reilly Media.

[7.1] Michael A. Salsburg. "What's All the Fuss About I/O Virtualization?" Posted online at http://www.cmg.org/measureit/issues/mit42/m_42_2.html, June 2007.

[7.2] Gautam Shroff. 2010. *Enterprise Cloud Computing: Technology, Architecture, Applications*. Cambridge: Cambridge University Press.

Index

Note: Page numbers in *italics* refer to figures, those in **bold** to tables, those that are underlined to charts.

abstraction software layer
  between hardware and operating
    system, 157–158, *158*
  as high-level programming language
    virtual machine, 158, *159*
  operating system and application, 158,
    159
active users, 78, 80, <u>81</u>, 81
additional CPUs, and CPU bottleneck
    models, 100, <u>101</u>, 105
additional disks, and I/O bottleneck
    models, 107, <u>109</u>, 112
additional servers, and CPU bottleneck
    models, 100, *102*, <u>102</u>, 105
AIX operating system, 27, 120, 202
algorithms
  application, and system overhead, 120
  load balancing, 193, 205, 214
  scheduling, 116, 117
  software, 21, 122, 127–128, 130–131,
    155
analytical method in closed queuing
    models, 38
APM (application performance
    management) vs. IT department
    business optimization, xi–xii
AppCapacity**Xpert** (OPNET), **47**
application algorithms and system
    overhead, 120
application customization, 178
application deployment, 178
application instrumentation, xiii

application log files, 88, 90–91, *91, 92,*
    93
application performance management vs.
    IT department business
    optimization, xi–xii
application scalability, 3–4, *4, 5,* 94–95,
    203. *See also* scaling
application sizing, xi, xii–xiii, **xiii,** xiv,
    2, 7, 8–9, 14, 173
  benchmarks, use in, 182–186, **184,**
    185
  empirical approach, 173–177, **174,**
    <u>175</u>, **175,** <u>176</u>, **176,** <u>177</u>, 193
  and hardware, 13, **13**
  model-based approach, 173–180, **174,**
    <u>175</u>, **175,** <u>176</u>, **176,** <u>177</u>, **179,** *180,*
    181, *182,* 182–186, **184, 185,** *187,*
    188–189, **190, 191,** *192,* **192,** 193
  time/cost constraints in, 82
  and virtualized hosts, 169–172, **169,**
    <u>170</u>, **170,** <u>171</u>
  and workload, 57–58, 59, 60, 61, 62,
    68
application tuning, xi, xii–xiii, **xiii,** xiv,
    2, 7, 8–9
  time/cost constraints in, 82
  tuning parameters, 120, 125, 126,
    127–130, *128, 129,* 131, 155
  and workload, 57–58, *58,* 59, 60, 61,
    63, 68
application workload. *See* workload
    characterization

Solving Enterprise Applications Performance Puzzles: Queuing Models to the Rescue,
First Edition. Leonid Grinshpan.
© 2012 Institute of Electrical and Electronics Engineers. Published 2012 by John Wiley
& Sons, Inc.

Printed and bound by CPI Group (UK) Ltd, Croydon, CR0 4YY

27/10/2024

14580272-0004